D0848849

Bloom's Modern Critical Interpretations

Bloom's Modern Critical Interpretations

Jane Austen's
Emma
New Edition

Edited and with an introduction by
Harold Bloom
Sterling Professor of the Humanities
Yale University

BLOOM'S
LITERARY CRITICISM
An imprint of Infobase Publishing

Bloom's Modern Critical Interpretations: Emma—New Edition

Copyright © 2010 by Infobase Publishing

Introduction © 2010 by Harold Bloom

Bloom's Literary Criticism
An imprint of Infobase Publishing
132 West 31st Street
New York NY 10001

Library of Congress Cataloging-in-Publication Data
  Jane Austen's Emma / edited and with an introduction by Harold Bloom.
    p. cm. — (Bloom's modern critical interpretations)
  Includes bibliographical references and index.
  ISBN 978-1-60413-816-0
  1. Austen, Jane, 1775–1817. Emma. I. Bloom, Harold. II. Title. III. Series.
  PR4034.E53J36 2010
  823.7—dc22

                          2009042264

Bloom's Literary Criticism books are available at special discounts when purchased in bulk quantities for businesses, associations, institutions, or sales promotions. Please call our Special Sales Department in New York at (212)967-8800 or (800)322-8755.

You can find Bloom's Literary Criticism on the World Wide Web at
http://www.chelseahouse.com

Cover design by Alicia Post
Composition by IBT Global, Troy NY
Cover printed by IBT Global, Troy NY
Book printed and bound by IBT Global, Troy NY
Date printed: February 2010
Printed in the United States of America

10 9 8 7 6 5 4 3 2 1

This book is printed on acid-free paper.

Contents

Editor's Note

My introduction argues for *Emma* as Jane Austen's masterwork, on the basis of Emma's dangerous yet wonderful imagination and her Shakespearean will-to-heroism.

Miss Bates and Mr. Woodhouse, the fools of *Emma*, are analyzed by Maaja A. Stewart, while Barbara Z. Thaden explores why Emma, and not the admirable Jane Fairfax, is the novel's heroine.

Susan Morgan uncovers the romantic affinity between Mr. Knightley and Emma, which is a turning outward toward the world.

The novel's last pages are seen by Sarah Emsley as an epithalamium, but then, as she remarks, so is the entire book.

Isobel Grundy defends the verbal excess, Shakespearean throughout, of Austen's grand talkers, after which John Wiltshire reads *Emma* as a romance of health and comfort.

Harriet Smith is defended by Ivor Morris as an exemplar of decency and pleasant kindness, while Juliet McMaster praises Emma's restless search for far horizons.

In this volume's final essay, Laura Mooneyham White speculates on the effect of the gypsy presence on the meaning of *Emma*.

HAROLD BLOOM

Introduction

Sir Walter Scott, reviewing *Emma* in 1815, rather strangely compared Jane Austen to the masters of the Flemish school of painting, presumably because of her precision in representing her characters. The strangeness results from Scott's not seeing how English Austen was, though the Scots perspective may have entered into his estimate. To me, as an American critic, *Emma* seems the most English of English novels and beyond question one of the very best. More than *Pride and Prejudice*, it is Austen's masterpiece, the largest triumph of her vigorous art. Her least accurate prophecy as to the fate of her fictions concerned *Emma*, whose heroine, she thought, "no one but myself will much like."

Aside from much else, Emma is immensely likable, because she is so extraordinarily imaginative, dangerous and misguided as her imagination frequently must appear to others and finally to herself. On the scale of being, Emma constitutes an answer to the immemorial questions of the sublime: More? Equal to? Or less than? Like Clarissa Harlowe before her and the strongest heroines of George Eliot and Henry James after her, Emma Woodhouse has a heroic will and, like them, she risks identifying her will with her imagination. Socially considered, such identification is catastrophic, since the Protestant will has a tendency to bestow a ranking on other selves, and such ranking may turn out to be a personal phantasmagoria. G. Armour Craig rather finely remarked that "society in *Emma* is not a ladder. It is a web of imputations that link feelings and conduct." Yet Emma herself, expansionist rather than reductionist in temperament, imputes more fiercely and freely than the web can sustain, and she threatens always, until she is enlightened, to dissolve the societal links, in and for others, that might allow some stability between feelings and conduct.

Armour Craig usefully added that "*Emma* does not justify its heroine nor does it deride her." Rather it treats her with ironic love (not loving irony). Emma Woodhouse is dear to Jane Austen, because her errors are profoundly imaginative and rise from the will's passion for autonomy of vision. The splendid Jane Fairfax is easier to admire, but I cannot agree with Wayne Booth's awarding the honors to her over Emma, though I admire the subtle balance of his formulation:

> Jane is superior to Emma in most respects except the stroke of good fortune that made Emma the heroine of the book. In matters of taste and ability, of head and of heart, she is Emma's superior.

Taste, ability, head, and heart are a formidable fourfold; the imagination and the will, working together, are an even more formidable twofold and clearly may have their energies diverted to error and to mischief. Jane Fairfax is certainly more *amiable* even than Emma Woodhouse, but she is considerably less interesting. It is Emma who is meant to charm us and who does charm us. Austen is not writing a tragedy of the will, like *Paradise Lost,* but a great comedy of the will, and her heroine must incarnate the full potential of the will, however misused for a time. Having rather too much her own way is certainly one of Emma's powers, and she does have a disposition to think a little too well of herself. When Austen says that these were "the real evils indeed of Emma's situation," we read "evils" as lightly as the author will let us, which is lightly enough.

Can we account for the qualities in Emma Woodhouse that make her worthy of comparison with George Eliot's Gwendolen Harleth and Henry James's Isabel Archer? The pure comedy of her context seems world enough for her; she evidently is not the heiress of all the ages. We are persuaded, by Austen's superb craft, that marriage to Mr. Knightley will more than suffice to fulfill totally the now perfectly amiable Emma. Or are we? It is James's genius to suggest that while Osmond's "beautiful mind" was a prison of the spirit for Isabel, no proper husband could exist anyway, since neither Touchett nor Goodwood is exactly a true match for her. Do we, presumably against Austen's promptings, not find Mr. Knightley something of a confinement also, benign and wise though he be?

I suspect that the heroine of the Protestant will, from Richardson's Clarissa Harlowe through to Virginia Woolf's Clarissa Dalloway, can never find a fit match because wills do not marry. The allegory or tragic irony of this dilemma is written large in *Clarissa,* since Lovelace, in strength of will and splendor of being, actually would have been the true husband for Clarissa (as he well knows) had he not been a moral squalor. His death cry ("Let this expiate!") expiates nothing and helps establish the long tradition of the Anglo-American novel in which the heroines of the will are fated to suffer either overt calamities or else happy unions with such good if unexciting men as Mr. Knightley or Will Ladislaw in *Middlemarch*. When George Eliot is reduced to having the fascinating Gwendolen Harleth fall hopelessly in love with the prince of prigs, Daniel Deronda, we sigh and resign ourselves to the sorrows of fictive overdetermination. Lovelace or Daniel Deronda? I myself do not know a high-spirited woman who would not prefer the first, though not for a husband!

Emma is replete with grand comic epiphanies, of which my favorite comes in volume 3, chapter 11, when Emma receives the grave shock of Harriet's disclosure that Mr. Knightley is the object of Harriet's hopeful affections:

> When Harriet had closed her evidence, she appealed to her dear Miss Woodhouse, to say whether she had not good ground for hope.
>
> "I never should have presumed to think of it at first," said she, "but for you. You told me to observe him carefully, and let his behavior be the rule of mine—and so I have. But now I seem to feel that I may deserve him; and that if he does choose me, it will not be any thing so very wonderful."
>
> The bitter feelings occasioned by this speech, the many bitter feelings, made the utmost exertion necessary on Emma's side to enable her to say in reply,
>
> "Harriet, I will only venture to declare, that Mr. Knightley is the last man in the world, who would intentionally give any woman the idea of his feeling for her more than he really does."
>
> Harriet seemed ready to worship her friend for a sentence so satisfactory; and Emma was only saved from raptures and fondness, which at the moment would have been dreadful penance, by the sound of her father's footsteps. He was coming through the hall. Harriet was too much agitated to encounter him. "She could not compose herself—Mr. Woodhouse would be alarmed—she had better go;"—with most ready encouragement from her friend, therefore, she passed off through another door—and the moment she was gone, this was the spontaneous burst of Emma's feelings: "Oh God! that I had never seen her!"
>
> The rest of the day, the following night, were hardly enough for her thoughts.—She was bewildered amidst the confusion of all that had rushed on her within the last few hours. Every moment had brought a fresh surprise; and every surprise must be

matter of humiliation to her.—How to understand it all! How to understand the deceptions she had been thus practising on herself, and living under!—The blunders, the blindness of her own head and heart!—she sat still, she walked about, she tried her own room, she tried the shrubbery—in every place, every posture, she perceived that she had acted most weakly; that she had been imposed on by others in a most mortifying degree; that she had been imposing on herself in a degree yet more mortifying; that she was wretched, and should probably find this day but the beginning of wretchedness.

The acute aesthetic pleasure of this turns on the counterpoint between Emma's spontaneous cry, "Oh God! that I had never seen her!" and the exquisite comic touch of: "she sat still, she walked about, she tried her own room, she tried the shrubbery—in every place, every posture, she perceived that she had acted most weakly." The acute humiliation of the will could not be better conveyed than by "she tried the shrubbery" and "every posture." Endlessly imaginative, Emma must now be compelled to endure the mortification of reducing herself to the postures and places of those driven into corners by the collapse of visions that have been exposed as delusions. Jane Austen, who seems to have identified herself with Emma, wisely chose to make this moment of ironic reversal a temporary purgatory, rather than an infernal discomfiture.

MAAJA A. STEWART

The Fools in Austen's Emma

As Henry James has said, "no 'story' is possible without its fools."[1] They form a stable and simple background through which and often against which the enlarging and intensified consciousness of the hero or heroine charts its course. In comic works, in particular, the fools respond, often in extreme fashion, to the basic conflicts and expectations of their worlds while remaining quite unconscious of the deeper human realities underlying these conflicts. To define the kind of fools a comic world generates, therefore, is to define a central aspect of that world. Whatever other complexity a comedy may have, the fools are traditionally conceived in simple outlines: rarely do critics disagree about the functions of the Sir Epicure Mammons or the Sir Wilfull Witwouds in comedy. Therefore, the diverse, sometimes radically opposed, evaluations of two of Austen's fools in *Emma*—Mr. Woodhouse and Miss Bates—is unusual enough to warrant our attention.[2] Because Austen's art fulfills, in so many ways, conventional expectations, her transformation of these conventions can remain submerged, even when these tranformations are basic to her method.

These two fools are in themselves simple, predictable characters with clear literary lineages.[3] Miss Bates derives from the innumerable portraits of the comic old maids whose pretensions are measured against their limitations in their varied misuses of language in worlds where a precise and complex

From *Nineteenth-Century Literature* 41, no. 1 (June 1986): 72–86. © 1986 by the Regents of the University of California.

idiom often gauges a character's potential to survive and succeed. Sometimes the fools function as blocking characters who are easily subverted through their own vanities: Lady Wishfort in *The Way of the World*, Mrs. Western in *Tom Jones*, or Madame Duval in *Evelina*. At other times, as aging women who express their sexual nature without arousing sexual desire, they are merely present to help create the comic atmosphere. Such traditional figures of fun are Mrs. Slipslop in *Joseph Andrews*, Mrs. Malaprop in *The Rivals*, and Tabitha Bramble in *Humphry Clinker*. Mr. Woodhouse's comic lineage is less clear, although his literary lineage is obvious: he resembles most strikingly the retired and impotent father figures who are given sentimental emphasis even in comic fictions and who are marked by unimpeachable moral superiority and a fearful withdrawal from the world as they try to immobilize their "daughters" into their own image: Mr. Villars in *Evelina* and Mr. Andrews in *Pamela* are examples of this type.

Austen's transformation of these type-figures is simple: she renders her old maid with a humanity that adds sympathy to our laughter, and she removes the sentiment from the fearful father, thus allowing us openly to see the comic possibilities precisely in those aspects that in earlier renderings of this type established his moral superiority: his retirement from the world and his attempt to convince his lively daughter to do the same. In spite of these changes, these two figures remain simple in their outlines in *Emma*. But Austen gives these simple figures complex connections with the world of Highbury, using them to delineate the deep as well as the superficial realities that surround the heroine. With care and precision she modifies the context around them, so that by the end of the novel we do not respond to them as we did at the beginning. This modification centers, of course, in the changes in Emma's enriching consciousness during the year in which she comes of age. In order to talk about the fool figures and their function, therefore, we have to talk extensively about the heroine herself.

Emma at the beginning of her story tries to establish structures of hierarchy. Not only does she insist on dividing the Highbury world into first, second, and third sets, but she also possesses all the conventional drives of the comic protagonist toward secular power and success that are traditionally rendered by images of dominance: the penetration of the secrets of others and the simultaneous preoccupation with legacies or with heiresses. Markedly, at the end of the novel, both of these measures of dominance are in Emma's grasp: she has become the repository of the secret story of each of the other characters, and she marries the most important and richest man in her milieu. But she turns from these secrets with weariness, relinquishing this drive for power as irrelevant to the deeper reality of her own life and accepting that the mysteries of other selves will remain impenetrable, when even the reactions of one of the simplest characters, Harriet, remain "unaccountable" and "unintelligible" to Emma.[4] Similarly, her marriage to Mr. Knightley recalls the traditional increase in status granted to the comic protagonist, although money and the power of status it confers are clearly pushed to the background. Her continuing residence at Hartfield, where she had always been the mistress of the house, serves to underplay her change in status. It is the field of the heart that has changed, with added emotional depth, greater generosity of spirit, having become both more contained within itself and potentially more open to the interactions with the rest of Highbury. Thus Emma ends her story at a point where conventional and secular criteria for success, so common in traditional comedy, yield to deeper movements of the spirit. No longer does she think predominantly in terms of hierarchy but instead in terms of relationships. The structure of her valuations no longer rests on an ascending and descending scale that tries to establish precise distinctions between good, better, best, but her interest now is to spell out similarities and differences, substitutions and transformations in the items that make up her life and her relationships with others.

Mr. Woodhouse and Miss Bates perform at the heart of this radical shift of emphasis. Emma's interaction with Miss Bates explicitly measures the psychological and moral development of the heroine. The climax of Austen's *Emma* is marked, as many critics have recognized, by the scene at Box Hill in which the heroine carelessly insults Miss Bates (p. 335).[5] This act shocks Emma out of her self-indulgent posture, leads her to try to establish a selfless relationship not only with Miss Bates but also with Jane Fairfax, and forms a prelude to her recognition of the meaning of Self in relationship to the Other as her nature yields itself to love.

The Box Hill scene, however, is not an isolated instance of the importance of Miss Bates as a complex reflector to Emma. Miss Bates, along with Jane Fairfax, is one of the two women who function centrally in Emma's drama, becoming in some ways far more important than the two women, Mrs. Weston and Harriet, whose relationships with Emma are explicit. The lines that connect Emma to the aunt and the niece are submerged to a level below the external action, involving the action that does not occur but should. Throughout most of the novel Miss Bates and Jane Fairfax are kept at a distance from Emma, a distance consciously and wrong-headedly fashioned by Emma herself. Early in the novel she rejects both the comparison Harriet institutes between herself and Miss Bates and the natural and equal association Mr. Knightley urges between her and Jane.

In rejecting the aunt and the niece, Emma rejects a woman's realm that seems to be marked by lack, negation, and limitation. These two women define a woman's lot not by what is but what is not, not by presence but by absence.

The aunt Emma dismisses as "so undistinguishing and unfastidious" (p. 77); the niece, although undoubtedly fastidious and elegant, maddens Emma with her conversation filled with "general approbation and smoothness" and in which nothing is "delineated and distinguished" (pp. 150–51). The aunt fits into the Highbury world by being a general approver, totally caught up in the trivial details of the lives of those around her, whereas the niece represents the need to hide her inner self from social judgment because of a striking lack of concurrence between nature and destiny. In her lack of independence her fortitude and resolve are directed toward accepting "sacrifice . . . penance and mortification for ever" (p. 147). Emma, whose own self-assured voice is marked by distinguishing and judging and who does not learn about "penance and mortification" until she reaches the end of her story, shrinks from the responses to the world that their destinies have encouraged.

The emphasis on limitations and lacks occurs strikingly in the set formal description of Miss Bates that appears in the third chapter of Book One of *Emma*, although she herself does not enter the dramatic scene until the beginning of the second book. Her importance is marked by this early appearance, through description, which occurs long before her presence in action. The first part of this description paints a bleak picture of a spinster who lives and cares on the margins of security:

> [She] enjoyed a most uncommon degree of popularity for a woman neither young, handsome, rich, nor married. Miss Bates stood in the very worst predicament in the world for having much of the public favour; and she had no intellectual superiority to make atonement to herself, or frighten those who might hate her, into outward respect. . . . Her youth had passed without distinction, and her middle of life was devoted to the care of a failing mother, and the endeavour to make a small income go as far as possible. (pp. 17–18)

This passage is curiously misleading in its emphasis on the vulnerability of Miss Bates and in its suggestion that she might find herself in situations in which she could be called upon to "make atonement" or "frighten" others in an effort to maintain her place. Appearing as it does early in the novel before the Highbury world has become manifest to us, this description suggests that the atmosphere in *Emma* will be the kind of dangerous atmosphere familiar to us in an English comedy of manners—a world of gossip and malice, of hypocrisy and vanity, where to reveal too much of oneself or to lack the skill to maintain one's position in society would be to lose at the rough game of social life in which the stakes are absolute. If Miss Bates had inhabited any of the works from Restoration comedies through Fielding and Sheridan and Burney's *Evelina*, she would indeed be "in the worst predicament in the world" because she would have the power of popularity without the power to subvert malice. She would also be rendered even more deeply ridiculous as an aging woman and an unmarried one. The guarded and defensive posture Emma herself assumes toward her world for most of the novel would be a correct posture in *The Way of the World* or *Tom Jones*, but as Emma learns, it does not attend to the deeper reality of her own world. For, indeed, we never see Miss Bates's vulnerability taken advantage of by the other characters, except for the one notable exception that occurs at Box Hill, when the antagonist she has no power to frighten turns out to be the heroine herself.

This initial description of Miss Bates sets up a relationship between the spinster and the heroine by echoing the sentence structure and the terminology of the initial description of Emma, but it is an echo that stresses difference and opposition. Whereas Emma is "handsome, clever, and rich" (p. 3), Miss Bates is "neither young, handsome, rich, nor married." This seemingly unqualified antithesis submerges the points of similarity between them: both are devoting their lives to the care of an aged parent, and neither entirely knows the impact she has on others. The similarity becomes increasingly more marked in the second part of the initial description of Miss Bates: Miss Bates, we are told, is a "happy woman," whereas Emma has a "happy disposition"; Miss Bates "thought herself a most fortunate creature, and surrounded with blessings in such an excellent mother and so many good neighbours and friends, and a home that wanted for nothing," whereas Emma has a "comfortable home. . . . a most affectionate, indulgent father," with her dead mother's place easily "supplied by an excellent woman as governess" (pp. 18, 3).

While Miss Bates thinks herself fortunate, Emma unquestionably is fortunate. But Austen suggests an unexpected reversal of our characteristic evaluation by intimating that Emma may be the one who lacks and Miss Bates the one who has. The happiness of Miss Bates is active and internal; the "happy disposition" of Emma remains only a potential one, not as yet actualized. Whereas Miss Bates is "quick-sighted to every body's merits" and has a "contented and grateful spirit . . . a mine of felicity to herself," Emma's happy disposition is refined into "a disposition to think a little too well of herself" (pp. 18, 4), and her requirement from the world is that it see no fault in her and hers. Miss Bates has both an "excellent" mother "and so many good neighbours and friends." In contrast, Emma's "excellent" human environment is restricted to kin and those who function as kin.

The second part of the initial description of Miss Bates leads us away from the world of malice and the sins of the tongue that set the atmosphere for most comedies of manners, and it depicts the unique world that Emma will finally recognize: the proper response to this world, in spite of its many limitations, involves not only acceptance but celebration. In other words, at the end of the novel Emma becomes more like Miss Bates rather than becoming more radically distinguished from her.

We can chart the changes in *Emma* by tracing through the novel the changes in a number of phrases that by contextual emphasis and by almost imperceptible modifications function the way metaphor and symbol function for other novelists in generating meaning. These phrases always sound casual within specific contexts, even general in their function as part of a specific description or reaction. But as they are repeated in the temporal sequence of unrepeatable events, their very recurrence, which suggests sameness, renders on a deeper level a difference of emphasis and meaning. Thus Emma's "happy disposition" and Miss Bates's "contented and grateful spirit" belong with a series of notations about dispositions and tempers in the search for the kind of temper that would yield happiness, a subject of Emma's intense meditations from the conclusion of Book One to the end of the novel. In a novel so singularly filled with characters who, we are told, have grateful, sanguine, mild, affectionate, contented, and unjudging dispositions that yield them happiness, Miss Bates is the epitome of such happiness, for her temper contains all these elements. Emma, who by the end of Book One is ready to decide that only simple people can be truly happy, has to find that she can modify her own happy disposition into a more complex version of Miss Bates's "contented and grateful spirit."

The second phrase, which is associated initially with both Emma and Miss Bates, undergoes a similar modification. "Not to find fault" characterizes Miss Bates as the total approver of all and Emma as requiring total approval by all. Initially it marks Emma's attempt to extend the atmosphere of her childhood environment to the rest of her world: her father is incapable of seeing Emma as anything but perfect, and Miss Taylor "had such an affection for her as could never find fault" (p. 4). The praise of her perfection that the larger world outside of the realm of affection can grant her, however, will belong to the trivializing, undistinguishing, and exaggerating social voice which will decide that Mr. Elton's bride has "every recommendation of person and mind; to be handsome, elegant, highly accomplished, and perfectly amiable" (p. 162)—and this before any at Highbury has met her. This is the kind of voice we hear as, in each of the three books, a different man responds to Emma's demand that no one find fault with her and hers. Even Emma hears the hollowness in Mr. Elton's chirpy repetition of "exactly so" in the comedy of errors in the first book. Emma, however, remains complacently deaf to the same hollowness in Frank Churchill's smooth verbal manipulation in the comedy of intrigue in Book Two. Although Frank is more sophisticated than Mr. Elton, his language, as he talks of Emma and all that belongs to her, is strikingly similar to the speech of the vicar, both by being punctuated with "exactlies" and "perfectlies" and also by its tendency to repeat Emma's own phrasings to convey total agreement and approval. This hollow approval comes to a climax in the third book where Mr. Weston, at Box Hill, momentarily assumes this function as he offers a conundrum on Emma's "perfection" to a hostile group a second after Emma has insulted Miss Bates and generally managed through her words and behavior to alienate most of the gathering. Since no one else is "disposed to command" after this climax of perfection, Mr. Weston's granting Emma what she sought breaks up the group, which has already been strained beyond a breaking point, isolating Emma herself as the alienated outsider.

It is left to the one man who does from the beginning "find fault" to forge the transformation of this phrase in Book Three, a transformation anticipated by Emma's tendency to test what she calls "love" by this phrase: to her relief, for instance, she decides that she could not be in love with Frank, since she does see his faults (p. 237). With similar relief she dismisses Mrs. Weston's pairing of Mr. Knightley with Jane Fairfax when he finds fault with Jane (p. 259). Emma herself has always been ready to recognize her own faults, but she could not bear that others would also recognize them. After Box Hill, she is filled with an urgent need to convey to three other characters—Mr. Knightley, Miss Bates, and Jane Fairfax—that she repents bitterly and openly her faults. This leads to the kind of moral development that coincides with the transformation of the phrase "to find no fault" into a more human and humane "faultless in spite of all her faults" (p. 393) with which Mr. Knightley expresses his love for Emma.[6]

The transformation of the defensive, vulnerable, and finally sterile image of "to find no fault" into the richly humble and vulnerable "faultless in spite of all her faults" combines with another transformation of phrase, one that is connected with Mr. Woodhouse. The differences in the connotations of the phrase "to be safe at Hartfield," which we hear throughout Book One, and of the transformed phrase "Hartfield was safe" if protected by the brothers Knightley (p. 440), which we hear at the end of the novel, reinforce the transformation of the world of the novel. Although the phrase "to be safe at Hartfield" emanates from Mr. Woodhouse, it is repeated by complex characters like John Knightley and Emma herself in Book One to mark the ego's retreat from a world of change and complexity into a seemingly invulnerable space.

The image of Hartfield as a place that will afford the necessary safety suggests the nature of Emma's reality in Book One. Her own retreat into the closure of family and kin is externalized by the oppressive and intrusive presence of Mr. Woodhouse in this initial book; either through reference or action, he crops up in sixteen out of the eighteen chapters, always circumscribing, always resisting energy and life. He seems to immobilize Emma—around him her wit misfires, her movement is controlled, and, in that memorable carriage ride of Mr. Elton's proposal, she is shut up in a small embarrassed space because "the fears of Mr. Woodhouse had confined them to a foot pace" (p. 120). Ceremonious, slow, ponderous, and obsessive, he stands at the center of the mental world defined by repeated words and phrases like "perfection," "safety," "to find no fault," and "always."

After the first book, however, the mood defined by Mr. Woodhouse sinks imperceptibly into the background. He is still present and he still complains and demands, but his presence no longer feels oppressive and limiting. What would have been impossible in Book One, now becomes relatively easy: Emma suffers little limitation as she goes to the Coles's party, to the ball at the Crown, and to the excursion at Box Hill, "provided all was safe at Hartfield." The fact that this represents Emma's change of response to her father rather than being a change in Mr. Woodhouse himself is made clear by details which would have felt inconceivable in Book One: in Book Three, for instance, we casually hear that Emma had replaced the small uncomfortable table at Hartfield with a modern round table some time in the unspecified past. With the memory of the mood of Book One still with us, we realize with some surprise that Emma's more energetic sense of what she wants must always have won out over her father's most formidable resistance, for he surely must have resisted such a change in his dining space, the center of his obsessions with ceremony and food.

Austen marks this shift of mood at the beginning of Book Two by giving Mr. Woodhouse an expression of empathy that is totally unexpected, not because it is out of character, but because we would not expect him to express it with quite so much delicacy and human understanding: "It is a great pity," he says, thinking of Miss and Mrs. Bates, "that their circumstances should be so confined! a great pity indeed! and I have often wished—but it is so little one can venture to do—small, trifling presents" (p. 153). If the inhabitants of Highbury give Miss Bates the pork loins, apples, and attention she needs in order to survive, they do so not condescendingly but with a memory of the dark stairway she has descended as a woman unprotected, incapable of doing anything herself to alter her external destiny. Mr. Woodhouse knows what Emma so easily forgets, that she is one of them, not a social inferior.

Never again does Mr. Woodhouse step out of his usual ponderous and ceremonious humors, but the moment is sufficient to relax the tension we were beginning to get used to in Book One and which we will largely cease to experience. Mr. Woodhouse does not change, but this passage functions to mark the point at which Austen ceases to use him to stress restrictions and limitations. Whereas in Book One he is ready to disperse the Christmas party at the Westons the moment they stop eating, in Book Three he comfortably settles in at the party at Donwell Abbey. Although in the first book his "courtesy" to others is expressed by suggestions to Mr. Knightley that he would have done better to have stayed home rather than visited Hartfield or by his attempts to stop all from eating the Westons' wedding cake, in the last two books we do experience a fine, simple courtesy in his warmth toward Jane, which makes even her relax, and in his ceremony toward Mrs. Elton, for, he says, "a bride, especially, is never to be neglected. More is avowedly due to *her*" (p. 252). Again, he knows instinctively that truly courteous behavior requires that we act toward others as their situation in life demands, not as we might feel toward them as individuals.[7] But Emma learns this painfully only after she forgets the demands of Miss Bates's situation at Box Hill.

Austen similarly reevaluates Miss Bates when Emma herself no longer finds her limiting but has learned to relish her rich and human presence. Although most readers find Miss Bates's monologues the amusing rendering of a great bore and willingly grant her sympathy long before Emma is ready to do so, they can also see why she should be so irritating to Emma. In the final scenes between Emma and Miss Bates, this irritation is wholly missing, partly because of the relief we feel with Emma that Miss Bates totally accepts her even after her unforgivable insult, but also because Austen suddenly deepens Miss Bates's monologue with an unexpected ability to generalize and abstract: talking about Jane, she says, "When one is in great pain, you know one cannot feel any blessing quite as it may deserve" (p. 343). As with Mr. Woodhouse, when she reassumes her usual humors, we listen to her with attention and interest after this, feeling no oppressive weight of the trivia.

To Mr. Woodhouse, other people's reality is reduced as his memory reduces Frank's letter: "Exceeding good, pretty letter, and gave Mr. and Mrs. Weston a great deal of pleasure. I remember it was written from Weymouth, and dated Sept. 28th—and began, 'My dear Madam,' but I forget how it went on; and it was signed 'F. C. Weston Churchill.'—I remember that perfectly" (p. 87). Measures of time and space, ceremonies and formalities for him surround a core of affection and the pleasures of affection. It is Miss Bates's function to fill in the blanks with the trivial and human details that Mr. Woodhouse's memory excludes. Her monologues bring a whole community of people into this novel that to the heroine—and to most readers—seems thinly populated. They also bring in a world of plenitude of unsorted details. With people and words, Miss Bates cherishes and connects, seemingly without discrimination, in a novel in which the heroine's initial endeavor is to distinguish and judge and separate. In this, Emma is like her father, who tries to separate and disjoin even those who belong to his own family, which is seen in his inability to accept Isabella's life as wife as well as a daughter; in his attempt to exclude Mr. Knightley from the first evening of the John Knightleys' Christmas visit; and in his unceasing mourning for the "poor Miss Taylor," who he thinks ideally belongs at Hartfield. The first time we see Miss Bates and Mr. Woodhouse together in a dramatic scene, we hear the principle of connection and the principle of separation strongly contrasted. Reacting to Elton's marriage, she says, "It is such a happiness when good people get together—and they always do," while he "lament[s] that young people would be in such a hurry to marry—and to marry strangers too" (pp. 156, 158).

Although Mr. Woodhouse's positive functions are restricted to his courtesy and to Emma's patient affection, which throws such good light on her in the midst of her arrogance and wrongheaded complacency, all of Miss Bates's functions conjoin to express the deepest movement in the novel, the movement that makes this novel such a powerful one: the transfusion of religious energy into daily thought and action. When she expresses gratitude to Mr. Woodhouse for a gift of pork loin, for instance, a deeper spiritual gratitude, reflected in her phrasing, flows naturally into Miss Bates's daily speech: "Our lot is cast in a goodly heritage" (p. 155).[8] Her gratitude emanates from the spirit, not merely temper or disposition. It flows out of that part of Christianity that says that the deepest worship is to love life as a gift of God. Her reiterated and comic expressions of gratitude to all her "good neighbours" are also, more deeply, expressions of a human stance toward a cosmos in which "everything [is] so good." Hers is a total thankfulness and a total celebration of a world where all gifts are undeserved and all gifts are freely given. As Emma learns, her neighbors must never simply "confer obligation" on her, as she herself has done, but give to her what they can as part "of a regular, equal, kindly intercourse" (p. 341), for her gratitude is not an expression of social humility to social superiors, which can demean both the giver and receiver, but an expression of trust in "so many good neighbours and friends," which is part of her trust in life itself as a gift of God.

Miss Bates, therefore, forms the dramatized center to the spiritual energy that informs the secular existence, an energy always present in this novel but initially dormant and unrecognized. The careless daily speech that attends only to the immediate situation early in the novel seems to sap the precise Christian meaning from recurring words like "evil," "temptation," "mortification," "forgiveness," and "penance" because the context in which they occur seems to be so insistently merely social. By the end of the novel, however, in the sequence beginning after Box Hill, the context changes to accommodate spiritual meaning. When, for instance, at the end of Book One, Emma withdraws momentarily from the world to gather her strength, we hear, "she wanted, rather, to be quiet, and out of temptation" (p. 130); the last word could be analogous to "enticement to act wrongheadedly" in its wholly secular context. At the end of the novel, however, when Emma thinks that, with Harriet's marriage to the sensible Robert Martin, her former protégée "would be never led into temptation" (p. 438), the language of the Lord's prayer has infused Emma's mind. Similarly, in Emma's "dreadfully mortifying" insight that the brothers Knightley understood Mr. Elton better than she did and in Mr. Woodhouse's insistence that they must not "disappoint and mortify the Coles" by refusing their invitation, the word "mortifying" signifies nothing more than social embarrassment. In contrast, the mortification, contrition, repentance, and penance that Emma feels after Box Hill—these words pile up one after another in the chapters that follow—have recovered their Christian meanings. Emma does feel a thorough and sincere change in her disposition, accepts her action as a sin of the spirit, feels both helpless in her personal guilt but is also eager to submit voluntarily to suffering and punishment to atone for that guilt. Emma, in short, is ready to come of age.

No longer does she simply react to the immediate situation in which a social embarrassment becomes mortifying, but she acts within a deepening consciousness of time wherein her failure to sustain a reciprocal relationship with others demands mortification. Until the episode at Box Hill, spatial relationships seemed more important than temporal ones. After Box Hill the image of space converts imperceptibly into the image of time: in the carriage driving away from Box Hill she "continued to look back, but in vain; and soon, with what appeared unusual speed, they were half way down the hill, and every thing left far behind" (p. 340). The past which cannot be retrieved, may be redeemed: "If attention, in future, could do away the past, she might hope to be forgiven" (p. 341). The conditionals and subjunctives that dominate her thoughts mark her movement away from the simpler imperative mood with which her story began. The modal "might" with its nervous uncertainty replaces the modal "must" with its arrogant certainty that desire and reality coincide.[9]

Only after Emma has recognized the reality of Miss Bates does she recognize her own reality. Only by recognizing that what seems to be lack functions centrally to the life of the spirit can Emma recognize her real desire, a desire easily satisfied by her world. What Austen says of Mr. Knightley typifies Emma's relation to her reality: "The affection, which he had been asking to be allowed to create if he could, was already his!" (p. 392). The slow hesitation in the repetition of phrases voicing uncertainty is subordinated to the direct simplicity of the main clause: "The affection . . . was already his.[10] The structure of the plot of the novel involves a similar uncertainty as subordinate materials perplex the clarity of the main design: strikingly, all three relationships that are consummated in marriage at the end of the novel were

established before the novel began." The consummation comes to Jane and
Harriet when inner desire is reconciled with the public realm; for Emma it
comes when inner desire surfaces in her consciousness. This self-conscious
redemption of everyday life the two fools could never share, but both are
active in transforming a thinly populated and superficially felt world (that we,
together with Emma, experience at the beginning of the novel) into a richly
filled, fulfilling, and courteous world in which the life of manners reflects the
life of the spirit. Emma may remain, as many readers have felt, a difficult, even
impossible woman who will need Mr. Knightley to keep her within bounds.
Her ending in marriage that depends on so many chance occurrences may
even seem deeply sad for those who feel that Emma has no possibility of
dramatically living out the insights she has had in the last chapters of the
novel. No other character in the novel, not even Mr. Knightley, really appreci-
ates what has happened to Emma. For what Austen has rendered is a deeply
spiritual drama that only the reader can share—the drama of a human being
who pushes back the specter of the meaninglessness of life, initially through
defensive denials of the actualities of her life, and who perceives "expectations" that invariably come to nothing. Only after deep suffering does she
realize the only way this specter of meaninglessness can be held at bay—by
the recognition that what she really needs has always been hers.

Notes

I owe a debt of gratitude to Harold M. Weber, Professor of English, University
of Alabama, for reading and commenting on an early version of this essay.

1. *The Art of the Novel: Critical Prefaces*, introd. Richard F. Blackmur (New
York: Scribner's, 1934), p. 67.

2. The controversy started with Sir Walter Scott's review of *Emma* in the
Quarterly Review, 14 (1815), 188–201. An excerpt is reprinted in the Norton Critical
Edition of *Emma*, ed. Stephen M. Parrish (New York: Norton, 1972), pp. 367–69.
Scott found the fools tiresome. For the opposite reaction, see Richard Simpson's
unsigned essay in the *North British Review*, 52 (1870), 129–52, rpt. as "Richard
Simpson on Jane Austen," in *Jane Austen: The Critical Heritage*, ed. B. C. Southam
(London: Routledge and Kegan Paul, 1968), pp. 241–65. For more recent negative
readings, see Marvin Mudrick, *Jane Austen: Irony as Defense and Discovery* (Princeton, NJ.: Princeton Univ. Press, 1952), pp. 190–96; and Ronald Blythe, introd.,
Emma (Baltimore: Penguin Books, 1966), p. 15. For recent positive readings, see
John Bayley, "The 'Irresponsibility' of Jane Austen," in *Critical Essays on Jane Austen*,
ed. B. C. Southam (London: Routledge and Kegan Paul, 1968), pp. 1–20, see esp.
pp. 4–7; and Lionel Trilling, introd., *Emma*, Riverside ed. (Boston: Houghton Mifflin, 1955), pp. xvii–xxiv.

3. Critics who have studied Jane Austen's originality by considering the tradi-
tion in which she wrote have recognized that this approach brings rich results. See F.
R. Leavis, *The Great Tradition* (London: Chatto and Windus, 1948), p. 5; A. Walton
Litz, *Jane Austen: A Study of Her Artistic Development* (London: Chatto and Windus,

1965); Frank W. Bradbrook, *Jane Austen and her Predecessors* (Cambridge: Cambridge Univ. Press, 1966); Kenneth L. Moler, *Jane Austen's Art of Allusion* (Lincoln: Univ. of Nebraska Press, 1968); and Alistair M. Duckworth, *The Improvement of the Estate: A Study of Jane Austen's Novels* (Baltimore: Johns Hopkins Univ. Press, 1971).

4. *Emma*, ed. David Lodge, Oxford English Novels (London and New York: Oxford Univ. Press, 1971), pp. 437, 438; subsequent quotations in my text are to this edition, which is substantially that of R. W. Chapman's with his emendations reconsidered.

5. See, e.g., Duckworth, *The Improvement of the Estate*, p. 155; and Bayley, "The 'Irresponsibility' of Jane Austen," p. 7.

6. These words recall Mirabell's about Millamant in William Congreve's *The Way of the World*: "For I like her with all her faults; nay, like her for her faults" (*A Treasury of the Theatre*, ed. John Gassner, rev. ed. [New York: Simon and Schuster, 1963], I, 434), and anticipate Vernon Whitford's about Clara Middleton in George Meredith's *The Egoist*: "Whatever she did was best. That was the refrain of the fountain-song in him, the burden being her whims, variations, inconsistencies, wiles" (*The Egoist*, ed. Robert M. Adams, Norton Critical Edition [New York: Norton, 1979], p. 250). All these statements recall Meredith's definition of the comic spirit as an ability to see the folly in those we love without loving them less.

7. I owe this idea to Bayley's fine discussion in "The 'Irresponsibility' of Jane Austen," pp. 6–7.

8. R. W. Chapman, in his "Notes" on *Emma*, refers the reader to Psalms 16.7 in the Prayer Book version: "The lot is fallen unto me in a fair ground: yea, I have a goodly heritage" (see *Emma*, Vol. 4 of *The Novels of Jane Austen*, 3rd ed., 5 vols. [London and New York: Oxford Univ. Press, 1933], p. 491).

9. Since writing this essay, I have read two excellent articles on Austen. The first is on her use of modals: Zelda Boyd, "Jane Austen's 'Must': The Will and the World," *Nineteenth-Century Fiction*, 39 (1984), 127–43. The second is specifically on *Emma*: Adena Rosmarin, "'Misreading' *Emma*: The Powers and Perfidies of Interpretive History," *ELH*, 51 (1984), 315–42.

10. I owe this idea to Elsie Michie, Newcomb College, personal communication.

BARBARA Z. THADEN

Figure and Ground:
The Receding Heroine in Jane Austen's Emma

*E*mma has long been considered Jane Austen's most perfectly executed novel (Bradley 380) and its heroine interpreted as being sympathetic in spite of herself, or, as Knightley puts it, "faultless in spite of all her faults" (*Emma* 298). Even those, such as Marvin Mudrick and John Hagan, who distrust the extent of Emma's moral regeneration, still find the character sympathetic though flawed. However, a close comparison of Emma with Austen's other heroines will reveal that Emma was not intended to be or to become a sympathetic character.

While some critics have discussed the striking dissimilarities between Emma and other Austen heroines, few believe that Austen did not sympathize with Emma, and many refer to a famous comment by J. E. Austen-Leigh: "She was very fond of Emma, but did not reckon her being a general favourite; for, when commencing that work, she said, 'I am going to take a heroine whom no one but myself will much like'" (204). Appreciating Emma as she was appreciated by her author has become something of a test of literary taste, as Reginald Farrer had already suggested by 1917: "A real appreciation of *Emma* is the final test of citizenship in [Austen's] kingdom" (380). But perhaps the "heroine whom no one but myself will much like" is not Emma Woodhouse at all. Austen-Leigh's comment suggests that this quotation, which does not name the heroine, is his only support for his supposition that

From *South Atlantic Review* 55, no. 1 (January 1990): 47–62. © 1990 by the *South Atlantic Review*.

Austen liked Emma. There is no other record of Austen actually having said this. In addition, Austen supposedly made this statement upon commencing *Emma*. We should consider it possible that *Emma* originated in Austen's mind with the heroine being not Emma Woodhouse, but Jane Fairfax, the character who bears Austen's name and who is much more like all her author's other heroines.

Critics occasionally admit that Jane Fairfax is superior to Emma Woodhouse. Wayne Booth, for example, claims that "any extended view of [Jane Fairfax] would reveal her as a more sympathetic person than Emma herself. Jane is superior to Emma in most respects except the stroke of good fortune that made Emma the heroine of the book" (249). Susan Morgan states that "in terms of fictional conventions we would most expect Jane Fairfax to be the heroine of *Emma*" (73); however, "we don't know Jane's mind or heart at all" (77). But even those who acknowledge Jane's superiority claim she is simply thrown into the background to show us Emma's faults and eventual regeneration; Emma alone is to have our sympathy. Perhaps Jane was to have had our sympathy all along, and our job as readers is to resist Emma's charm.

The novel opens with the famous statement, "Emma Woodhouse, handsome, clever, and rich . . . had lived nearly twenty-one years in the world with very little to distress or vex her" (1). Readers of Austen's three previously published novels would automatically be alerted that they are now in a different world, or rather the same world viewed from an entirely different perspective. Emma is at the pinnacle of her society, with no inducement to marry or to change her position, unlike Elinor Dashwood, Elizabeth Bennet, and Fanny Price. Emma is practically her father's only child, she has the complete run of the household, she has charmed everyone in her circle, she receives nothing but flattery and compliments from her father and her governess, and she has the power to avoid anyone who does not care to flatter her.

All of Austen's other heroines are more or less oppressed. In fact, it seems that a primary characteristic of an Austen heroine is that she feel somehow different from her family. Even Elizabeth Bennet, the character who most resembles Emma, is not in a position of power in her household. She and Jane are qualitatively different from Mrs. Bennet and the three younger daughters, and Elizabeth is constantly made to suffer for her moral superiority and sensitivity, as are Elinor Dashwood, Fanny Price, and Anne Elliot. James Thompson points out that Elizabeth Bennet and Anne Elliot are "rescued from an abusive family and translated to the prince's palace" (160). Although Emma would like to feel that she is her father's superior, they are very much alike. They begin the novel together and, significantly, end it still together; every other Austen heroine must, as Thompson points out, abandon her family, not reintegrate with it (160).

Unlike any other heroine, Emma has also been "doing just what she liked" (1) for her entire life, and her constant and only concern is herself. Austen's other novels reserve such freedom and selfishness for unsympathetic characters. Robert Ferrars, in *Sense and Sensibility*, selfishly does just as he likes and remains a perennial favorite with his set. Mrs. Norris's favorite Maria Bertram does just what she likes whenever her father is not around, while Mary and Henry Crawford have even more freedom, and Anne Elliot's older sister Elizabeth selfishly does just as she likes with her father's complete approval. Elizabeth Elliot is, in fact, introduced in terms very similar to those describing Emma: "For one daughter, his eldest, [Sir Walter Elliot] would really have given up any thing, which he had not been very much tempted to do. Elizabeth had succeeded, at sixteen, to all that was possible, of her mother's rights and consequence; and being very handsome, and very like himself, her influence had always been great, and they had gone on together most happily" (37). Austen's heroines, on the other hand, are usually characterized by restraint and self-effacement. Elinor Dashwood, Fanny Price, and Anne Elliot are quiet and decorous, while Elizabeth Bennet, though not usually self-effacing, is certainly restrained when among her superiors and much less concerned with herself; she is honestly capable of caring and working for someone else's welfare.

Emma also feels that her town "afforded her no equals" (2), an attitude Austen usually reserves for characters hopelessly incapable of regeneration, such as Mrs. Ferrars, Lady Catherine de Bourgh, and Sir Walter Eliot. As long as Elizabeth believes that Darcy possesses this attitude, she abhors him. However, even Darcy has always admitted that he had equals—he only had to be convinced to admit Elizabeth among them. Emma, like other characters who believe in their own superiority, feels justified in her condescension, especially towards Harriet, just as Mrs. Ferrars condescends to Elinor, Lady Catherine to Elizabeth Bennet, Mrs. Norris to Fanny, and Sir Walter Elliot to the Crofts. While other Austen heroines must suffer this type of condescension, Emma practices it.

The pride of class is far from being accepted in any other Austen novel, nor does it characterize any other Austen heroine. Elizabeth Bennet, for example, is willing to accept Wickham as an admirer, and Anne Elliot marries beneath herself in terms of rank, while all the heroines marry up in financial terms. The basic plot of an Austen novel seems to involve a heroine who must attract her man, not because of her social position, but in spite of it. Her intrinsic merits must attract the man who can see through class markers or surface appearances; only one Austen heroine, Emma, has "sufficient resources to marry into the class into which she was born" (Thompson 140). Socially superior men and women also must prove their intrinsic worth in a classic Austen plot; Darcy will not be accepted for his wealth and position alone, Georgiana must prove that she is not the snob everyone reports her to be, and Bingley must prove worthy of Jane's love, not merely capable of her support. This intrinsic worth plot is of course the plot of romance, and the reader should realize very early in *Emma* that she is not reading a romance at all. Emma need prove her intrinsic worth to nobody, and she knows it.

While the typical Austen heroine is somehow different from the other members of her milieu, Emma is consistently shown as having character- istics similar to many other characters in the novel. Her relationships with other people are early shown to be, like Frank Churchill's and Mrs. Elton's, those of a self-centered egotist. Emma is isolated not because she is superior but because she must feel superior; she cannot participate in a relationship where she is not *first*. In this characteristic she exceeds both Mrs. Elton and Mrs. Norris.

Although it seems that Mr. Knightley is the only person who dares to criticize Emma throughout the novel, this is because his is the only criticism she will listen to and therefore the only criticism we hear. He is not, as is often thought, a standard of correct thinking, because he is from first to last completely charmed by Emma Woodhouse, as she well knows. He admits that he has been charmed by her, and in love with her, since she was "thirteen at least" (319), and she reveals that she has always known she was *first* with Mr. Knightley (285). No, Knightley is not the impartial critic that Emma needs, nor is he the lover who will "do her good" by giving her "some doubt of a return" (26).

Emma has managed to charm everyone in the novel and most of the readers of the novel, but, as Mudrick points out,

> Charm is the chief warning signal of Jane Austen's world, for it is most often the signal of wit adrift from feeling. The brilliant facades of Emma and Frank Churchill have no door. Indeed the only charming person in all of Jane Austen's novels whom both she and the reader fully accept is Elizabeth Bennet, and Elizabeth has obvious virtues.... The other heroines—Elinor Dashwood, Catherine Morland, Fanny Price, Anne Elliot—are presented in the quietest colors. And Willoughby, Wickham, Mary Crawford, Frank Churchill—the charming interlopers—always betray. (201)

Mudrick's perceptive account of charm has one flaw, however; Elizabeth Bennet, who seems so similar to Emma, is *not* charming. Charm, as Mudrick points out, is a surface quality that hides an empty mind and a shallow soul. Elizabeth Bennet lacks it—she knows she is not as beautiful as her sister Jane, she never counts on being first in any situation, and she never depends on her beauty, her charm, or her position in society for anything. In fact, Darcy's first impression of her is negative, and he refuses to dance with her. But Elizabeth Bennet has wit, a quality of mind Darcy only gradually comes to appreciate. Her wit, intelligence, and good sense are very different from Emma's surface brilliance.

While Elizabeth's worth is gradually revealed to Darcy, Emma's shallowness is revealed to the reader, and to Knightley, but the latter is too charmed to notice. Emma claims that "till it appears that men are much more philosophic on the subject of beauty than they are generally supposed; till they do fall in love with well-informed minds instead of handsome faces, a girl, with such loveliness as Harriet, has a certainty of being admired and sought after" (42). Like many of Emma's statements, this one also applies more to herself than anyone else. When Jane Austen turns from romanticism to realism, as she does in every novel, she admits that a good many men (and women) marry for beauty and/or money, and only a few marry for intrinsic worth. Emma has beauty, money, and charm, all she needs to be eminently successful in Jane Austen's world. While such romances as Emma and Knightley's have usually been relegated to subplots in Austen's novels, this novel relegates the Jane Fairfax "intrinsic worth" plot to the background and foregrounds the "realistic" relationship.

A version of this plot had appeared in the three previously published novels. In *Sense and Sensibility*, Edward Ferrars is initially attracted to Lucy Steele, who has nothing to recommend her other than beauty and charm. He comes to his senses after a long engagement and marries the sensible girl, Elinor. But lest we think that life is always like this, Austen reminds us that it is not in almost every other marriage in the novel. Robert Ferrars is flattered into marrying Lucy Steele, showing how "an unceasing attention to self-interest, however its progress may be apparently obstructed, will do in securing every advantage of fortune, with no other sacrifice than that of time and conscience" (364). Willoughby marries only for money, "but that he fled from society, or contracted an habitual gloom of temper, or died of a broken heart, must not be depended on—for he did neither" (367). John Dashwood continues to love his "angel" Fanny, and Colonel Brandon never ceases being infatuated with Marianne despite her flightiness and rudeness and never turns his eyes to the more stable Elinor, even though Elinor herself admits that there is no reason in the world to assume that Marianne is the better choice between the two of them, based "on an impartial consideration of their age, characters, or feelings" (328).

Mr. Bennet has been "charmed" into marrying a very silly woman in *Pride and Prejudice*, and it may be that Lydia has used some similar charms on a temporarily lax Wickham. In *Mansfield Park*, Lady Bertram "had the good luck to captivate Sir Thomas Bertram" because her beauty counterbalanced the fact that she was "at least three thousand pounds short of any equitable claim" to him (41), and Edmund Bertram falls in love with the charming Mary Crawford. Only the unlucky elopement of his sister, at the right moment, prevents Edmund from declaring his love to Mary. If Edmund had married Mary Crawford, we would have had a novel similar to *Emma*. Fanny Price would not have been considered a suitable mate for the same reasons Jane Fairfax is not considered suitable—they are a few thousand pounds short of deserving these men, but they are also too "reserved."

Other Austen heroines, in the process of proving themselves worthy, must suffer the consequences of their actions, but, as P. J. M. Scott points out, Emma is always turning "the other person's cheek" (70), especially Harriet's. Elinor Dashwood, Elizabeth Bennet, Fanny Price, Anne Elliot, and other sympathetic characters, such as Jane Bennet, Jane Fairfax, and even Marianne Dashwood, undergo a severe trial period between the time they realize their love and the time they are offered (or accept) their marriage proposals. Emma, on the contrary, has only to realize that she loves Knightley, and to let him know it, to receive her marriage proposal.

Readers not completely spellbound by Emma's charm probably agree that Emma has negative qualities not possessed by any other Austen heroine. However, most readers believe that Emma has matured and improved by the end of the novel—if not completely, then at least enough to deserve Mr. Knightley. Hagan's article offers a useful summary of critical opinions on the quality of Emma's regeneration, and he himself claims that a total moral regeneration in Emma would detract from the realism of the book; both Emma and Knightley remain flawed because they are not paragons of virtue but "delightfully human" (35). It seems that few critics feel justified in creating a truly "hard school" of *Emma* criticism, not because the novel itself does not offer sufficient evidence for such an interpretation, but simply because coming up with a motive and a strategy for such a novel on Austen's part seems impossible. However, there may be sufficient evidence to justify a reading that finds an unregenerate Emma maintaining her preeminence by marrying a charmed Knightley, the theme being an anti-Romantic acceptance of a shallow, materialistic society.

The Box Hill episode, for example, is often pointed to as a turning point in Emma's character development. Emma has been goaded into high-spirited repartee by Frank Churchill's too obvious flirtations and has been led into a *faux pas*, one she does not even notice until Knightley rebukes her for being cruel to Miss Bates. Emma is mortified to learn she has "exposed herself to such ill opinion in any one she valued" (258)—the "anyone" being, of course,

Knightley and not Miss Bates. But Knightley's motivation for this rebuke, it turns out, is not simply pointing out the demands of noblesse oblige: "He had been in love with Emma, and jealous of Frank Churchill, from about the same period, one sentiment having probably enlightened him as to the other. It was his jealousy of Frank Churchill that had taken him from the country.—The Box Hill party had decided him on going away" (298). Knightley's primary reason for rebuking Emma is to bring her "down" from this high-spirited flirtation—to burst her private bubble, of which he is jealous. Emma is mortified, as any aspirant to the pinnacle of society would be when rebuked by the acknowledged head of that society, ironically called *High*bury to emphasize the motivations of the major characters.

While Emma pays lip service to Knightley's criticisms because the obligation of kindness to social inferiors fits nicely with her perception of her own superiority, there are many indications that by the end of the novel she has changed little. For example, Emma begins by despising her supposed inferiors ("the Eltons were nobody" 92) and ends the novel with the same attitudes. Her objection to Harriet's possible marriage with Knightley is based largely on social standing: "Such an elevation on her side! Such a debasement on his!" (284).

Emma also begins the novel insisting on being first in everything. She had been horrified at the idea of Knightley's loving Jane Fairfax, not only because this would have been "a very shameful and degrading connection" (152), but also because then there would be a "Mrs. Knightley for them all to give way to!—No—Mr. Knightley must never marry" (154). And at the end of the novel, these are Emma's "regenerate" feelings on realizing that she did indeed love Knightley:

> Till now that she was threatened with its loss, Emma had never known how much of her happiness depended on being first with Mr. Knightley, first in interest and affection. Satisfied that it was so, and feeling it her due, she had enjoyed it without reflection; and only in the dread of being supplanted, found how inexpressibly important it had been. Long, very long, she felt she had been first. . . . She had herself been first with him for many years past. (285)

Emma's love of Knightley is based not so much on his qualities as on her fear of no longer being first in Highbury and in a friend's estimation.

Emma has inadequacies similar to those of a heroine in an early fragment, "Catherine," who "professed a love of Books without Reading, was Lively without Wit, and generally good humoured without Merit" (Chapman, *Works* 198). Emma adopts Harriet because she needs a foil to hide her intellectual and moral inadequacies and realizes that Jane Fairfax would certainly not answer. She selects another young woman, one who could not possibly outdo her in anything, and is horrified to find this young woman threatening to supplant her in social standing. Once Knightley proposes, Emma no longer needs a foil, and she can calmly ship Harriet off to London, as she would now be only a "dead weight" (310). The friend she had supposedly been trying to advance will now sink into oblivion; all social connections between them will gradually be severed.

From the very first sentence describing her, Mrs. Elton is introduced as a parody of Emma: "The charming Augusta Hawkins, in addition to all the usual advantages of perfect beauty and merit, was in possession of an independent fortune, of so many thousand as would always be called ten" (122), a parody, of course, of the first sentence in the novel. But this element of parody does not diminish by the end of the novel. Mrs. Elton's reaction to Emma's marriage is that a Mrs. Knightley would "throw cold water on everything" (324), just as Emma had believed that "A Mrs. Knightley for them all to give way to" would be insufferable—unless that Mrs. Knightley were herself. And one of the last comments in the novel is Mrs. Elton's, on the shabbiness of Emma's wedding. The two will be forever rivals in Highbury society, battling over who is more superior or more necessary "to enliven a country neighborhood" (190); however, Emma, as usual, has gained the advantage.

Emma's other parody is Frank Churchill, who has "used everybody ill—and they are all delighted to forgive him" (295). Emma herself finally admits that she and Frank are similar in their destinies (331). Both are rich, spoiled, supremely imaginative, charming, good-looking, entirely unrestrained in their games, and potentially harmful to people with less power than themselves. Both know intuitively that, whatever they do, they will not come out losers. The only lives that Frank and Emma can ruin are other people's. They themselves are blessed with every advantage, including a happy disposition and a never-failing ability to be pleased with themselves.

Jane Fairfax, on the other hand, is the traditional Austen heroine "growing up with no advantages of connection or improvement to be engrafted on what nature had given her in a pleasing person, good understanding, and warm-hearted, well-meaning relations" (109). Like Elizabeth Bennet, Jane must endure the constant company of well-meaning but socially despised and ludicrous relatives. Like Fanny Price, she must endure silently while a flirt of high social standing plays with the man she loves. She also displays the diffidence necessary to her social position, a reserve that makes her unattractive to so many readers.

However, all of Austen's heroines display this diffidence, reserve, and iron self-control when they find themselves in a position of dependence or powerlessness, as well as when they are with people with whom they have nothing in common. Elinor Dashwood displays such behavior not only with Mrs. Ferrars (her superior) but also with Lucy Steele (with whom no true communication is possible). Elizabeth Bennet only seems lively and unreserved because she is so often in the company of Jane, with whom she feels at ease, but with Lady Catherine de Bourgh she weighs her words, and to her sister Lydia she is a "prig." We must accept that the only alternative to being diffident and reserved, in Jane Fairfax's social position, is being like Harriet or like Miss Bates. A person of inferior social standing can only be lovable in Austen's social world by making a public display of inferiority, and this is something Austen's heroines resolutely refuse to do.

But why, if Austen considered Jane Fairfax the heroine of her novel, is Jane given almost no attention and Emma made the titular and actual heroine? Perhaps a partial answer can be found in "Plan of a Novel, According to Hints from Various Quarters," which, according to Chapman, Austen wrote about 1816, when she was finishing *Emma*. It involves a "heroine of faultless Character herself—perfectly good, with much tenderness & sentiment, & not the least Wit—very highly accomplished ... particularly excelling in Music" whose friendship is "sought after by a young Woman in the same Neighborhood, of Talents & Shrewdness, with light eyes & fair skin, but having a considerable degree of Wit. Heroine shall shrink from the acquaintance" and be pursued by "some totally unprincipled & heart-less young Man, desperately in love with the Heroine" who is "often reduced to support herself and her Father by her Talents & work for her Bread;—continually cheated & defrauded of her hire, worn down to a Skeleton, & now and then starved to Death. . . . The name of the work *not* to be *Emma*—but of the same sort as S&S and P&P" (Chapman, *Works* 428–30). Austen here is satirizing the classic romantic plot of the oppressed heroine, which she must have felt naturally drawn towards, but she had always realized, and perhaps at age thirty-nine realized still more, just how romantic these plots were.

Austen had always had one eye focused squarely on an unpleasant social reality, as most of her subplots and minor characters demonstrate. Every novel contains characters who are either born with wealth and rank and think any other attainment unnecessary, or who attain peaks of social and economic eminence by their charm, bombast, gall, deception, ruthlessness, personal attractiveness, or other qualities totally divorced from intelligence, talent, sensitivity, and morality. But these characters had always been painted with the bold, harsh, and spare strokes of the caricaturist.

Emma, it can be contended, is Austen's attempt to broaden the sphere of her characterization. It is an artistic exercise in characterization and a *tour de force* in ironic point of view. Austen perhaps realized by this time that her unsympathetic characters were mere caricatures, entertaining but unconvincing. While Austen herself (as her letters show) and all of her heroines are perceptibly outside the social mindset of their milieu and operate as critical observers of manners and mores, in *Emma* Austen attempts a view from within the "high" society that she herself does not particularly like. A character such as Emma (or Lucy Steele, or Robert Ferrars) must appear attractive to all those who accept her values, or she would not be so successful. She also must appear attractive to the reader in order to prove the point that charm is more convincing than virtue, morality, or merit.

D. W. Harding long ago expressed Austen's attitude towards society as "regulated hatred": "Her books are, as she meant them to be, read and enjoyed by precisely the sort of people whom she disliked. . . . she invites her readers to be just their natural patronising selves" (70). However, Austen's social position also made it imperative not to make too many enemies. Her way of dealing with her dissatisfaction with the social order is a precise and wry humor, not polemic.

Readers have long noticed the "careful and even guarded" nature of Austen's style (Thompson 13), although disagreeing on its cause or significance. While Thompson feels the guardedness is "historically determined," not a personal characteristic of Austen's (5), it may be argued that in *Emma* Austen is the outsider depicting the mind of an insider, Emma Woodhouse. Austen's letters reveal her as being much too conscious of everyone's faults and foibles, including her own, from a very early age to be an unconscious "insider." But her acerbic wit was kept under strict control. Austen-Leigh's *Memoir*, which depicts "gentle Jane" as a person who never satirized anyone in her life (114), gives some insight into the style of life to which Austen was accustomed. There was no privacy, and decorum was constantly maintained: "to lie down, or even to lean back, was a luxury permitted only to old persons or invalids . . . a model gentleman of his day . . . would have made the tour of Europe without ever touching the back of his travelling carriage" (52). This is the supreme self-control shown by all of Austen's sympathetic heroines. Austen's letters, even (or perhaps especially) after being severely censored by Cassandra Austen, encourage a view of the author, even as a young woman, as one who was always acting her proper role in family and society, who early assumed a mask of decorum and took it off to nobody, except perhaps occasionally to her sister Cassandra.

Jane Aiken Hodge, who develops this view in her biography of Austen, agrees that the Jane Austen we know from letters has no similarities to Emma Woodhouse: "Emma is practically everything that Jane Austen was not. Where Jane Austen was poor, shy, and one of eight, Emma is rich, spoiled, over-confident and to all intents and purposes an only child" (171).

Miss Mitford's famous second-hand description describes Austen as being far from charming, as having

> stiffened into the most perpendicular, precise, taciturn piece of "single blessedness" that ever existed, and that, till *Pride and Prejudice* showed what a precious gem was hidden in that unbending case, she was no more regarded in society than a poker or a fire-screen, or any other thin upright piece of wood or iron that fills its corner in peace and quietness. The case is very different now; she is still a poker—but a poker of whom every one is afraid. (Schorer xii)

Contemporary readers often accuse Jane Fairfax of being a "poker," and the charge has been leveled against Fanny Price, Anne Eliot, and even Elinor Dashwood. But Austen's letters and novels do not support a positive view of "charm," or a negative view of "diffidence." The history of criticism has shown, however, that it is in bad taste to dislike Emma. Jane Austen herself probably realized that an unmitigated attack on a "child of fortune" might seem like sour grapes and never herself admitted she did not like Emma, but her letters, like her novels, according to Virginia Woolf, have "a sense of meaning withheld, a smile at something unseen, an atmosphere of perfect control and courtesy mixed with something finely satirical, which, were it not directed against things in general rather than against individuals, would be almost malicious" (2: 276). And Woolf is probably right—Jane Austen did not personally dislike Emma, but she did wonder at the society that apotheosizes her.

Austen chooses to show us the world through Emma's eyes because she realized that a novel about Jane Fairfax might be so sentimental and romantic as to overpower her sense of humor entirely (some say this is true of *Mansfield Park*). So, the artistic thing to do in such a case was to adopt the opposite perspective to the one normally taken—the perspective of Emma Woodhouse. Booth asks us to imagine *Emma* told from Jane Fairfax's point of view, to imagine an unsympathetic Emma. But try to imagine *Sense and Sensibility* told from Mrs. Ferrars's point of view. Of course we would have an unsympathetic Elinor Dashwood—but would we have a sympathetic Mrs. Ferrars? The artistic challenge here (one George Eliot would take seriously to heart) is to imagine, and depict, a sympathetic Mrs. Ferrars (or Emma Woodhouse) who does all the nasty things the unsympathetic Mrs. Ferrars does. The effects on the novel are profound.

The first effect is that the quality of all other caricatures is softened. If the author begins with a caricature and turns her into a heroine, all the heroine's associates will be caricature types, yet they must be painted with a softer brush because they are the heroine's friends. Mr. Woodhouse is Mrs. Bennet from Lydia's point of view, or Sir Walter Eliot from Elizabeth Eliot's point of view. Mrs. Weston is Mrs. Norris from Maria Bertram's point of view. But what happens to those characters whom the heroine does not like is even more interesting. They simply cannot be turned into caricatures because they have all the qualities the author admires. They can be talked down by other characters, but they cannot be shown doing despicable things because they would not do them. In fact, *they cannot be represented at all.* It is amazing, as others have pointed out, how little we know of Jane Fairfax, how little we see her or hear her. When she appears on the scene she seldom talks, and the few times she does speak, as when she speaks about the "governess trade" that sells not human flesh but human intellect (204), she sounds like a character from an entirely different novel, and no one, of course, understands her in this one. She is the novel's "blind spot"—her story is conspicuously "absent" from the text. We are never allowed to understand her motivations as we are those of the subplot characters in other Austen novels. Fredric Jameson reminds us that registering such a "determinate and signifying *absence* in the text" can help us understand its structure by allowing us to "reestablish the series that should have generated the missing term" (137)—that series being of course the standard Austen plot. Occasionally, according to Jameson, an essential element of a text will be absent because the author does not want to be reminded of some unpleasant historical reality; this is Arnold Kettle's explanation—"Jane Austen has no answer" to Jane Fairfax (103).

In *Emma*, Jane Fairfax is "The Real—that which resists desire" and which is "fundamentally unrepresentable and non-narrative, and detectable only in its effects." It "can be disclosed only by Desire itself, whose wish-fulfilling mechanisms are the instruments through which this resistant surface must be scanned" (Jameson 184). When Austen moves away from romance, when she refuses the wish-fulfilling solution, she cannot represent her heroine at all. The fact that Jane Fairfax marries at all could be seen as a "containment strategy" whereby Austen diffuses "those impulses toward the future and toward radical change" (Jameson 193) by those who feel Austen is basically an apologist for the class structure. However, it is also an essential plot element, like Harriet's marriage, because it is essential for Emma's peace of mind in her "best of all possible worlds."

Emma (and many of Austen's other novels) has generated so many different interpretations because, as Alistair Duckworth points out, it has a "surplus of signification" (42). In *Emma* especially, we are never sure how much of the narrative is told from Emma's point of view and how much is Austen's commentary. We know (or think we know) that we are not in a totally subjective first-person narrative because occasionally we know things that Emma does not. However, readers constantly disagree as to whether a particular narrative passage is from Emma's point of view or the author's.[1] For example, David Spring believes Austen has "no great liking for social fluidity" because Emma criticizes Frank Churchill for his indifference to rank (55), and Janet Todd sees "the overwhelming presence of Jane Austen as narrator in all her books" (118). However, as this paper has argued, we seldom see Jane Austen anywhere, least of all in *Emma*. Woolf is right in believing Austen to be profoundly absent from her novels, giving them "a certain aloofness and incompleteness" (2: 76).[2] Duckworth would call this the criticism of "suspicion," a concept developed by Paul Ricoeur (Duckworth 42). However, in a letter written in 1808 about Egerton's *Fitz-Albini*, Austen herself writes, "*I* am not [disappointed], for I expected nothing better. Never did any book carry more internal evidence of its author. Every sentiment is completely Egerton's" (Chapman 32). This alone should warn us that every sentiment in an Austen novel will not be Austen's.

Perhaps humor was a form of defense for Jane Austen, a means of hiding an inner self that had no validity in her society. In Austen's world, love, marriage, and monetary security based on merit is the wish-fulfilling fantasy. It is pursued, but always hesitantly, in all of her novels. In *Emma*, she admits more than in any other novel that this is "perhaps incompatible with the facts of human existence" or at least of her social order. But, because Austen is a supreme stylist, in her art and in her life, she can laugh at herself and the world. Nietzsche once wrote that strong natures "enjoy their finest gaiety" under the compulsion and constraint of a self-imposed style (98–99). Austen's work does not depict anger, or passionate despair, or personal suffering, and this, as Woolf recognized, is not a weakness but Austen's greatest strength.

Notes

1. Much of the disagreement arises because of Austen's use of "Free Indirect Discourse," also known as "narrated monologue" and "style indirect libre." Louise Flavin summarized the various terms. Free Indirect Discourse occurs when a character's interior speech is "exactly transposed into narrative language, without explicit quotation or authorial explication" (Cohn 113). Flavin claims that Austen's increased use of Free Indirect Discourse in *Mansfield Park* "makes distinguishing FID from narrator comments difficult at times" (138). The difficulty is exacerbated in Austen's next novel, *Emma*. Hence it is impossible to maintain a steady perspective on which character is the "figure," or foregrounded character, and which is the "ground" against which we establish our perspective, as in the well-known ambiguous drawing of the vase that, if looked at again, becomes two profiles.

2. All Woolf quotes are cited from Todd, "Who's Afraid of Jane Austen?"

Works Cited

Austen, Jane. *Emma*. 1815. Norton Critical Edition. Ed. Stephen M. Parrish. New York: Norton, 1972.

———. *Persuasion*. 1818. Ed. D. W. Harding. New York: Penguin, 1965.

———. *Sense and Sensibility*. 1811. Ed. Tony Tanner. New York: Penguin, 1969.

Austen-Leigh, J. E. *A Memoir of Jane Austen*. London: Richard Bentley, 1870.

Bradley, A. C. "Jane Austen, a Lecture." In *Emma*. Norton Critical Edition. Ed. Stephen M. Parrish. New York: Norton, 1972. 376–80.

Bloom, Harold, ed. *Jane Austen's "Emma": Modern Critical Interpretations*. New York: Chelsea, 1987.

Booth, Wayne C. *The Rhetoric of Fiction*. Chicago: U of Chicago P, 1961.

Chapman R. W, ed. *Jane Austen's Letters to Her Sister Cassandra and Others*. 2nd ed. Oxford: Oxford UP, 1952.

———, ed. *Minor Works*. London: Oxford UP, 1954. Vol. 6 of *The Novels of Jane Austen*. 6 vols., 1953–1969.

Cohn, Dorrit. *Transparent Minds: Narrative Modes for Presenting Consciousness in Fiction*. Princeton, NJ: Princeton UP, 1978.

Duckworth, Alistair. "Jane Austen and the Conflict of Interpretations." In Janet Todd, ed. *Jane Austen: New Perspectives*. New York: Holmes & Meier, 1983. 39–48.

Farrer, Reginald. "Jane Austen." 1917. In *Emma*. Norton Critical Edition. Ed. Stephen M. Parrish. New York: Norton, 1972. 380–82.

Flavin, Louise. "*Mansfield Park*: Free Indirect Discourse and the Psychological Novel." *Studies in the Novel* 19.2 (1987): 137–59.

Hagan, John. "The Closure of *Emma*." In Bloom, Harold, ed. *Jane Austen's "Emma": Modern Critical Interpretations*. New York: Chelsea, 1987. 19–36.

Harding, D. W. "Regulated Hatred: An Aspect of the Work of Jane Austen." 1940. In Lodge, David, ed. *Jane Austen: "Emma," a Casebook*. London: McMillan, 1968. 69–73.

Hodge, Jane Aiken. *Only a Novel: The Double Life of Jane Austen*. New York: Coward, 1972.

Jameson, Fredric. *The Political Unconscious*. Ithaca: Cornell UP, 1981.

Kettle, Arnold. "Jane Austen: *Emma*." In Lodge, David, ed. *Jane Austin: "Emma," a Casebook*. London: McMillan, 1968. 89–103.

Lodge, David, ed. *Jane Austen: "Emma," A Casebook*. London: McMillan, 1968.

Morgan, Susan. "*Emma* and the Charms of Imagination." In Bloom, Harold, ed. *Jane Austen's "Emma": Modern Critical Interpretations*. New York: Chelsea, 1987. 67–100.

Mudrick, Marvin. *Jane Austen: Irony as Defense and Discovery*. Berkeley: U of California P, 1968.

Nietzsche, Frederick. "The Gay Science, 290." *The Portable Nietzsche*. Ed. Walter Kaufmann. New York: Penguin, 1976. 93–101.

Ricoeur, Paul. *Freud and Philosophy*. Trans. Denis Savage. New Haven, CT: Yale UP, 1970.

Schorer, Mark. Introduction. *Pride and Prejudice*. By Jane Austen. Riverside Edition. Boston: Houghton Mifflin, 1956. v–xxi.

Scott, P. J. M. *Jane Austen: A Reassessment*. Totowa, NJ: Barnes, 1982.

Spring, David. "Interpreters of Jane Austen's Social World." In Todd, Janet, ed. *Jane Austen: New Perspectives*. New York: Holmes & Meier, 1983. 53–72.

Thompson, James. *Between Self and World: The Novels of Jane Austen*. University Park: Pennsylvania State UP, 1988.

Todd, Janet, ed. *Jane Austen: New Perspectives*. New York: Holmes & Meier, 1983.

———. "Who's Afraid of Jane Austen?" In Todd, Janet, ed. *Jane Austen: New Perspectives*. New York: Holmes & Meier, 1983. 107–27.

Woolf, Virginia. *Collected Essays*. London: Hogarth, 1966.

SUSAN MORGAN

Adoring the Girl Next Door:
Geography in Austen's Novels

W hen I think about Jane Austen's *Emma*, and about what so affects me in this novel besides the sheer mental exuberance of its main character, I come to the plot. Jane Austen tells a great story. One reason I know that Austen was particularly fond of Emma, apart from her own explicit statement that "Emma is a character whom no one but myself will much like," is that she made Emma so much like herself. Emma Woodhouse and Jane Austen are both imaginists, both storytellers about other people's lives. Moreover, Austen certainly did not write a story in which Emma was required to give up her creativity, to see her clouds of glory, in Wordsworth's phrase, fade into the light of common day. Near the end of the story Emma can still claim persuasively that she always deserves the best treatment because she never puts up with any other. The resolution to Austen's plot does offer her beloved creation and fellow creator only the best treatment, which does not include having to give up her imagination. The real difference between the author and her flawed but fabulous heroine is that Austen tells a better story than Emma. And part of what's better is Austen's more inventive, and less conventional, vision of romance.

It is one of the great triumphs of *Emma*, the novel, that it is a love story about a young woman and the man who has lived next door to her for all of her life, in which for most of the narrative, and certainly for all the years that

From *Persuasions* 21, no. 1 (Winter 2000), unpaginated. © 2000 by the Jane Austen Society of North America.

they have been neighbors before the story opens, neither of them even notice that they have any such feeling for each other. She's a spoiled girl, he's been a fond but critical family friend. The families have been close, her sister even married his brother. My daughter, who is 12, has yet to have the pleasure of reading Austen's novels. You can see this lack in the oh-so-skeptical reply she offered a few days ago to a new friend of hers who asked her if she thought a certain boy was really cool. "Did you know, he wouldn't take off his snow boots for all of the second grade." Mr. Knightley and Emma would have known all about each other's habits in snowboots. And they still fell in love.

Austen holds our attention for most of the story with Emma's love plots, her speculations and machinations for other people. And we are riveted by it all. Then, near the end, Austen suddenly waltzes the romance between Mr. Knightley and his lively young neighbor onto her narrative stage, effectively upstaging the little dramas Emma has spun. And almost as suddenly, we realize that we are looking at a far superior style of matchmaking to any of Emma's inventions, that this is a much better kind of love story after all.

The plot of this novel is a tribute to everyday life, to the extraordinary richness of the world that is to be found in our very own neighborhoods, to the enormous potential for happiness that can be fulfilled by going no farther than right next door. I think one reason so many of us love this novel is that it celebrates the high possibilities, the real thrills, the enthusiastic creativity and even the "perfect happiness" to be found in the small worlds of ordinary life in which almost all of us live.

What I want to talk about today is what the novel does not celebrate: a commitment to, a belief in, the superiority, both moral and aesthetic, of remaining in our small worlds, of choosing the sedentary and the circumscribed—whether that choice is based on fear or on ego. We need to be wary of our own tendencies, as readers and imaginists ourselves, to romanticize, to look at Hartfield and Highbury as some sort of charming portrait of an idyllic rural life. I want to look at *Emma* and its relations to Austen's other novels from what I am calling the perspective of geography. By that I simply mean where Austen's heroines are located and the range of their locations, how much they move around.

On even the most literal level, readers of Austen's novels know that her heroines usually do not stay in that "country village" Austen spoke of to Fanny, and often do not spend much time there at all. Let me just remind you of their mobility. *Northanger Abbey*, probably the earliest written of Austen's published novels, which actually came out posthumously together with *Persuasion*, sports a heroine who is on the road for almost all of the novel. Catherine Morland is introduced to us in Chapter One, and the narrator moves quickly from her infancy through age ten to seventeen. So much for her home life. She leaves home on the very first page of Chapter Two, and is delighted to do so. As I am sure you all remember, the rest of the novel is Catherine in the public world of Bath and then as a houseguest at Northanger Abbey. Finally, in Chapter Twenty-Nine, eleven weeks after her departure and with just three chapters left in her story, Catherine quite reluctantly comes home.

Of Austen's five other completed novels, three also begin with the heroine leaving home. At ten years old, Fanny Price is sent away from a nuclear family with too many children and too little money, to live with her relatives at Mansfield Park. She will never come home again, though she does return to Portsmouth for a visit when she is grown. *Sense and Sensibility* and *Persuasion* open with the heroines being literally forced out of their homes by the financial carelessness of their fathers, the Dashwood sisters when their father dies without leaving them any savings and their half-brother inherits their home, and Anne Elliot when the Elliot family must move to rented lodgings in order to pay their bills.

In other words, four out of six of Austen's completed novels offer, as the opening move of their plots, the heroine leaving home. In the earliest, and I would say the simplest, plot of the four, seventeen-year-old Catherine Morland goes cheerfully off to begin her adventures at being an adult, and returns home briefly at the end of the book. The next three versions are darker and more complex. They open with acute financial problems which result in the heroine regretfully leaving home. All three stories introduce a heroine forced out of the familiar and into the greater world. Nor do they simply move to another place and stay there, though Fanny Price comes closest to this. The Dashwood sisters, driven off by the heirs to their estate, will stay in their rented Devonshire cottage for only a part of the narrative. They soon travel to London and later to yet another country estate, Cleveland, before returning at the end of the book to their cottage. While Anne Elliot is given a brief visit back to Kellynch Hall, most of her story takes place in other houses and villages and towns, at Uppercross and Lyme and Bath. And even in *Northanger Abbey*, though the narrator explicitly states at the outset that the Morlands were not "poor," the heroine must leave her family behind and travel with a neighbor, in part because the largeness of her family makes it too expensive to make their own trip to Bath. Fanny Price may move around the least, but on the other hand her very entrance into the novel is as a child out of place, an exhausted "little girl [who] performed her long journey in safety."

My point is that all this changing around hardly adds up to a stable, in the sense of settled and static, domestic universe as the geographic setting of Austen's work. We can see clearly how Austen's own reluctant move from Steventon to Bath after her father retired, and then, after he died, her years of social wandering with her mother, her sister Cassandra, and her friend

Martha Lloyd before settling at Chawton, were the biographical basis for the mobile openings of Austen's plots.

But biographical explanations are not enough. If we are intent upon claiming that Austen's fiction offers representations of the narrow domestic sphere of upper class country females in regency England, we need to be very precise about where to locate that domestic sphere. In four of the six completed novels it is quite literally not to be found in the heroines' homes. Instead, I would say that what interests Austen, the moment at which the lives of young women become interesting to her, is precisely the moment when they, whether by choice or by economic force, leave the protection, the safety, and the sheltering innocence of their homes. When they move, and thus become changeable, their stories can begin. And for three out of four (the exception being Fanny Price), the traveling will continue, as the novels, along with their heroines, shift from place to place. Their geography is the geography of England.

It is time for us to acknowledge how vexed Austen's notion of home really is. And it is time for us to recognize just how often Austen's heroines move around, how frequently they seem detached from any particular one spot that can be called home, how many places in England they visit, how very itinerant they can be. One major component of the domestic lives Austen creates for her heroines is their lack of domesticity, their wandering feet, the way they are drawn outward, however often reluctantly at first, away from their private and insufficient homes and toward a beckoning larger social world.

The extent to which Austen's novels are infused with the social issues and public debates of Regency England, the myriad ways the novels take place in a public rather than in a private and domestic sphere, is not a new insight. Many readers of Austen's work have studied the ways in which her novels examine such topical issues as the economics of marriage and the rights of women, the aesthetic movement and the improvement of estates, theaters and amateur theatricals in the Regency period, and the role of the Royal Navy in British imperial enterprise. One of the most useful recent books to place Austen's work within the frame of the topics and issues which pervaded the public spaces of her age is *Jane Austen and Representations of Regency England* by Roger Sales. I found particularly exciting his discussion of the Regency obsession with invalidism, its links to ideas of leisure and consumption, and to the pervasive role of watering places in Regency society and in Austen's work. Mobility was certainly commonplace for country gentry in Austen's time. And the reasons for traveling are not hard to see. Given both the financial pressures to marry and the fashionable obsession with illness that Sales delineates, it was a kind of tourism which was virtually required of the men and women of Austen's class.

But Austen does not always tell her stories through the convention of departures. *Pride and Prejudice* is one of two Austen novels in which the heroine does not begin her story by leaving home. Elizabeth Bennet spends a great deal of the narrative ensconced in the family estate at Longbourn. I make just two quick points about this. First, I am hardly claiming that Austen's novels all have or should have the same pattern, but simply that a geographic range covering many locales around England is a central motif in Austen's novels. My second point has probably already occurred to all of you. Elizabeth may live at Longbourn with her family for most of her story, but she does, of course, leave home during the novel, taking two crucially significant journeys. In the first, the visit to the parsonage at Hunsford, she receives Darcy's marriage proposal and in the second, touring Derbyshire with the Gardiners, she sees Darcy on his home ground. Both trips are centrally important, operating as key moments in Elizabeth's process of changing the ways she has looked at and evaluated the world around her. The insights gained on those journeys are high points of the education in perception which will lead to Elizabeth's final journey: the move to marriage and to life at Pemberley.

Emma

And then there is Emma, the exception—as she would probably be pleased to hear—to all these patterns. It is hard to overstate the extent to which Emma does not move around, the narrowness of her physical sphere. She simply never goes anywhere. From the first page of her story to the last, Emma spends all her nights, and virtually all her days, comfortably in her own home. She does stroll the village and have dinner at the Westons. She attends a party at the Coles and a dance at the Crown, visits the estate adjoining Hartfield for the first time in many years, and even goes as far as Box Hill, for the first time in her life. That's about it. Geographically speaking, Emma remains solidly in the neighborhood of her own home.

What are we to make of this relentless immobility? Well, not only did Austen repeatedly use plot patterns of moving away from home as ways of educating her heroines in her other novels, I would say that she also did so in *Emma*. Emma's story, too, offers claims for the value of wider experience, of literal as well as perceptual movement out from the confines of self into the larger world. After all, this strikingly exceptional heroine is wrong for most of the novel, wrong in the personal and class snobbery that keeps her so geographically limited and wrong in the melodramatic conventionality of the romance stories she invents. The narrative point, surely, is that such stasis, and such certainty, are not particularly desirable. Emma should have left home, imaginatively if not literally, should have moved beyond the blindnesses attendant on her overly confined life. She and her sister have been shaped by a father who is committed to being an invalid, committed, that is, to sustaining the degree of power and control made possible through refusing ever to move outward from the small boundaries of the world you personally rule. Mr. Woodhouse, that gentle tyrant, has taught Emma well, has assured her of her superiority in the little world they dominate and has, through his very inaction, encouraged her in the belief that the only way always to be first is never to leave home.

Emma can be read, then, as a novel about geography, an extended debate between the forces for stasis and the forces for movement out to the regions stretching beyond our domestic sphere, each side struggling to persuade the young woman with "the power of having rather too much her own way, and a disposition to think a little too well of herself" to join their point of view.

The novel, after all, is full of movement, of repeated instances of traveling. With the exception of the Woodhouses and the Bates, no one seems to stand still. Since, through the narrative technique, we stand with Emma, we can only get reports about all the trips the other characters take. But those reports are almost continuous. Recollect that Frank Churchill seems to travel so much as to appear virtually adrift. As Mr. Knightley, suffering from stabs of jealousy, so sharply puts it, "'He cannot want money—he cannot want leisure. We know, on the contrary, that he has so much of both, that he is glad to get rid of them at some of the idlest haunts in the kingdom. We hear of him for ever at some watering-place or other'" (146).

Frank's conduct, in spite of Mr. Knightley's rather sniping account of it, reminds us that covering a lot of territory is not really the point, that one can move around with no more purpose than self entertainment—a goal the sedentary Emma is herself far too familiar with. On the other hand, it was on one of those trips to a watering-place, Weymouth, that Frank was so blessed as to get to know Jane Fairfax well enough to become engaged to her, clearly the best thing that could have happened to him. Thinking about Frank suggests that whatever an active geographical sense may mean in one of Austen's novels, that meaning is complex.

Yet not to move out to the world beyond Highbury is clearly a mistake, and probably an egotistical position to take. I want to emphasize how pervasive movement is in this story, how virtually everybody is doing it. Mr. Weston had traveled all over before settling at Randalls, both as a Captain in the militia and as a businessman. Jane Fairfax, of course, was orphaned as an infant, and in her third family before the age of nine. She has grown up traveling around with the Campbells, and her very presence in the story is as a temporary visitor whose next destination is unknown. Emma's sister, Isabella Knightley, for all she shares her father's fondness for the privileges and controls made possible by sickness and invalidism, does her share of traveling, not only living in London and visiting Highbury but even taking a vacation trip to the seaside. Mr. Knightley takes a sudden trip to London to avoid watching Emma flirt with Frank, a motive for travel in no way superior to Frank's popping into London to buy a piano for Jane. Even Harriet can make a significant journey, accomplishing in London what she did not in Highbury: seeing the dentist and accepting the hand of farmer Martin. And surely one sign of the ways Emma has moved out from the self-centered vision which distorted her better understanding for so much of the novel is that her plan at the end is precisely to travel a little, for she and Mr. Knightley to take as their honeymoon "a fortnight's absence in a tour to the sea-side" (483).

Clearly, then, leaving home, seeing something of a world beyond the neighborhood, is a major part of all of Austen's novels, including even *Emma*. It was, after all, a major part of Austen's own life. Geographic range, whether it took the form of trips to London, to Bath or Weymouth or Brighton, or to other family's estates, was typical behavior for the leisured gentry of Austen's time. One implication of this historical point is that one cannot define the domestic sphere, either in or out of Austen's novels, as somehow isolated or retired or set apart from public life. In fact, the line between private and public life, unless we mean by public those activities which were explicitly restricted to men, such as serving in Parliament or being in the militia or the navy or riding in horse races, becomes harder and harder to draw.

If the domestic sphere, or private life, takes place not only in girls' bedrooms or sitting rooms in their homes or in the back rooms of their dressmaker's shop, but also in the drawing room and at dinner parties at a whole range of houses in various counties of England, and also at the theater or in shops and carriages or on the street or in public rooms, perhaps in London or Bath or Lyme or Portsmouth; then that sphere is surely the sphere where everyone lives, men as well as women, and not some separate women's world. Austen's novels are certainly focused on young women who come from the rural gentry, but even in her limited number of narratives these young women go almost everywhere. Her novels are not set so much in domestic spaces as in social spaces: all the places where men and women, whether relatives, friends, acquaintances or strangers, meet and make connections and live their lives.

Geography and Politics

Emma's stasis, her geographic narrowness, is finally not sustainable either in the England in which Austen lived or in the England which she created. In terms of the plot, where the other characters often travel is precisely to Emma's enclosed little sphere. The movement of the action is like wave after wave of increasingly less manageable invasions of what Emma had considered her own turf. Mr. Elton and Harriet are more or less locals, it is true.

Then along come Jane and Frank, locals but surely from the larger world. And then Mrs. Elton, clamoring, often successfully, to take over Emma's position as first. There is no place, not even Hartfield, protected from the claims, and the possibilities, of the larger world.

Most of us would agree that Austen's visions of personal lives carry a political meaning. That meaning is usually discussed in terms of contemporary debates about women's rights. Roger Sales has argued that "the detail about the travel arrangements in *Emma*, together with the way in which much of it highlights relationships between mobility and power, needs to be seen as an important part of a political argument about the positioning of women" (162). He suggests that mobility is a kind of opportunity not open to women as it is to men. I would also suggest, somewhat differently, that mobility can as easily represent lack of power. Jane Fairfax has mobility because she travels with a Colonel and his family, not because she has the economic right to control her own location. Without money, Jane must move around as others dictate, while her equally impoverished relatives, Miss and Mrs. Bates, can't go anywhere. The narrative point is not that men have mobility and women don't but that both settling down and moving around involve money, and the social independence that economic independence can bring.

But money is not the only issue here. The politics of *Emma* are concerned in many ways with the position of women, with their economic and their social constrictions and, most eloquently, with their future possibilities. Both the constrictions and the possibilities are presented in generational terms, in Austen's insight that daughters are inheritors, and they may inherit a great many things besides an income. What they inherit adds a national dimension to Austen's debate about the future of her heroines. The question of what young women can and should become, cast in terms of what the past has to offer them, turns out to include a perspective on England's inheritances and possibilities as well.

A telling moment in *Emma* is when we are introduced to Jane's "inheritance." She is the daughter of a Lieutenant Fairfax who had died "in action abroad" (163), most plausibly in the Napoleonic Wars, her mother dying soon after and Jane left without financial or personal support. Jane's parents, the fighting lieutenant and the widow dead of grief, represent the values and sacrifices of an England caught up for more than two decades in the Napoleonic Wars. Jane is one of the multitude of casualties from those Wars. By 1814, the year Austen wrote *Emma*, the Wars had been defining national values for years in terms of active aggression and suffering. Paralleling this military view the novel also offers a civilian version, a sketch of those who watched the wars from home, represented by Emma's father. Mr. Woodhouse is as militant as any soldier in an invalidism which provides him with the victories possible through a policy of isolation. War without and a defensive isolationism based on fear, particularly fear of French invasion, within were the twin poles of British politics during the Napoleonic Wars. These are the two stances which the new generation received as a legacy of those wars. But in 1814, with Napoleon defeated and banished to Elba, peace looked possible at last. Fighting and isolationism looked like an inadequate inheritance, to shape a young woman or a nation.

The daughters who have inherited these legacies, Jane and Emma, must put them aside. Instead, they must forge a new form of relating to the larger public sphere, one which, I would say, can combine Jane's mobility with Emma's power to be creative. Jane, who has long since moved extensively in the larger world, will have restored, in extravagant measure, the one element the war had taken from her: the financial security to make her own decisions. And Emma will relinquish the false control inherent in living a confined life and join with Mr. Knightley to take a little trip out into the greater world. She will never become as far-ranging a traveler as Jane. Nor need she. For these new young women, and the new England they will help to make, all the chance for a future requires is the optimism to move outward and that right to make that choice themselves.

The joy of future peace which so animates this novel is seen in its hopes for young women's new choices and its hopes for a new national identity. Emma's personal move away from isolation without losing personal power also carries a possibility for England. The nation too needs to abandon attitudes of self-defensiveness, entrenched opinions and conservative identities, both about itself and about other nations. The novel argues for a personal politics of openness and expanding relationships. It argues for the possibilities, political as well as personal, international as well as domestic, in throwing off the protective insularity of the war years and engaging sympathetically with the ever interesting, ever expanding, wide wide world. That is the kind of geographic promise which Austen offers Emma, and which her novels are still offering to her readers.

And yet, and yet . . . , there remains something still to be said. Emma's story is hardly a simple hymn to the charms as well as the virtues of engaging with the larger peacetime world of Regency England. In terms of the love story, it is hard to see any significant reason for leaving home if what home can offer is Mr. George Knightley cheerfully dropping by.

That is surely part of Austen's point. Home is a wonderful place to be. But that was true at the very beginning of the novel, when Emma reigned at Hartfield, Mrs. Weston had just left to be married, and Mr. Knightley stopped by, bringing with him the affection of long years. Yet all this is not enough to bring Emma and Mr. Knightley together, for affection to be ignited into passion, or there would be no book to write. Both become aware of their love through jealousy, through thinking another might gain the heart of the person whom they had not even been aware they loved. They need Frank Churchill dashing around looking like such an appropriate beau, and Harriet finding romantic Mr. Knightley's kindness in asking her to dance, then speaking her admiration for him. Austen's radical argument is that for Emma and Mr. Knightley to find their happiness rural retirement is not enough. They need the help of the rest of the world.

Once a definition of home and of nation includes the imaginative geography required for women to acknowledge and then to participate in shaping a larger community, the way is cleared in *Emma* for the happy ending. This larger definition of home helps to explain the narrative function of one of the odder characters in this novel: the other brother, the doppelgänger Knightley, John. George and John are presented as notably alike, but with a fundamental difference. John argues, without the gentleness of Mr. Woodhouse (with whom he has more in common than he knows), for the old ways. He represents a domestic tyranny which reads only as "folly"—"people's not staying comfortably at home when they can" and announces with discomforting isolationist certainty that "'I never dine with any body.'" John, of course, has chosen control, with the larger world as a threat and home as a safety zone. And part of what makes home so safe is the presence of a dependent woman. Isabella, his wife, is appropriately the sister whose conversations can be ignored and whose decisions can be made for her.

The difference between the two brothers is that George Knightley has long since learned the charms of "not staying comfortably at home when [he] can." And thus he has come to love a far different kind of woman, a woman never loath to be first, a heroine who will never put up with being ignored and will never understand domesticity as keeping life cozy for a man. Mr. Knightley and Emma both, though he perhaps a little earlier than she, have come to appreciate not only themselves but also the life that lies outside their imaginations and their knowledge. And because they have, the two are capable of that beautifully liberated social and geographic solution to the problem of their romance: that as Emma's husband, Mr. Knightley will leave his home, and move into hers.

Works Cited

Austen, Jane. *Emma*. Ed. R. W. Chapman. 3rd ed. Oxford: OUP, 1969.

Sales, Roger. *Jane Austen and Representations of Regency England*. London: Routledge, 1996.

SARAH EMSLEY

The Last Pages of Emma: Austen's Epithalamium

At the Jane Austen bicentennial conference held at the University of Alberta in 1975, George Whalley gave a paper in which he suggested that Austen is a poet. In saying this he wasn't merely stating the obvious, which is that she did write verse, but instead he was arguing that it is something about the power of her prose that makes her a poet. He writes,

> I should like to suggest that Jane Austen is a poet in two senses: (a) in her craftsmanship in language; and (b) in the conduct of the action within each novel. In the first sense, we need to consider fine-grained detail with an ear alert to the dynamics of language; in the second, we are concerned with the disposition of forces within the whole universe of the novel, particularly that mutual definition of plot and character the product of which Aristotle called *drama*. (108)

The elements of the first sense he identifies as irony, precision, and the symbolic naming (rather than describing) of things; the second sense is the "realising of a stylised plot in probable action" (132). He admits that his argument "may be a bit dense," but says that the topic is "too simple to be anything but unmanageable" (109). Testing the full implications of Whalley's argument as it applies to the novels in general would be a lengthy

From *Persuasions* 23 (2001): 188–96. © 2001 by Sarah Emsley.

undertaking; for now I shall focus very specifically on the ending of *Emma*, which seems to me to bear a remarkable similarity to the poetic genre of the epithalamium, or marriage poem, despite the fact that it is prose.

The epithalamium is usually thought of as a classical or renaissance genre, with Edmund Spenser's "Epithalamion" (1595) as the most famous example in English. (There are a number of variants of the word—"epithalamium" and "epithalamia" are the Latin terms, with English versions such as "epithalamion" and "epithalamies," and, for a betrothal poem, "prothalamion.") During the renaissance revival of the genre, Spenser, Sidney, Shakespeare, Donne, Jonson, Herrick, Milton, Crashaw, Vaughan, and Dryden all composed epithalamia inspired by the wedding poetry of Sappho, Aristophanes, Euripides, Theocritus, Catullus, Statius, and Claudian. There were even a few medieval epithalamia, by Chaucer, Dunbar, Lydgate, and James I of Scotland. Highly formal and often quite formulaic—George Puttenham's *Art of English Poesie* (1689) and Julius Caesar Scaliger's *Poetices libri septem* (1561) provided guidelines for conventional composition—epithalamia usually praise the beauty and character of bride and bridegroom, talk about their families, and celebrate unity, stability, and harmony, sometimes incorporating traditional fescennine verses designed to ward off evil by poking fun at it, and invariably ending with blessings and benedictions.

Literally, the term "epithalamium" (from the Greek words *epi* + *thalamos*) refers to a song, often a kind of folk-song, sung outside the nuptial chamber, just before the consummation of the marriage, but as Virginia Tufte writes in *The Poetry of Marriage: The Epithalamium in Europe and Its Development in England* (1970), even in classical times poets "had begun to call almost any kind of wedding song or poem an epithalamium, and before long they applied the term to certain types of poetry and prose which dealt with subjects unrelated to marriage except in a metaphorical way" (3)—such as spiritual marriage or the union of two rivers (Spenser, "The Thames doth the Medway Wed"). The boundaries of the genre are not firm, and thus the term is not limited to poetry; therefore, whether the conception of Austen is expanded from novelist to poet, or the definition of the epithalamium is expanded to include prose as well as poetry, it is possible to see Austen as the author of an epithalamium. How, then, does the tradition of the epithalamium emerge in the ending of *Emma*, and why is it useful to think of Austen in this unconventional way?

Near the ending of the novel, as is conventional in the epithalamium, bride and bridegroom are individually and jointly praised. Emma enjoys "the animated contemplation" of "Mr. Knightley's high superiority of character" (480), and thinks of his worth as a "companion for herself" and as a "partner in all those duties and cares" (450); Mr. Knightley, for his part, thinks Emma the "sweetest and best of all creatures, faultless in spite of all her faults" (433), and praises his bride-to-be for the good influence she has had on Harriet Smith—Emma, like most brides, "submit[s] quietly to a little more praise than she deserved" (475). Both agree to the "'beauty of truth and sincerity in all [their] dealings with each other'" (446), and Mr. Knightley experiences "something so like perfect happiness, that it could bear no other name" (432). Significantly, Austen says of Emma that "*Her* change was equal" (432). Emma is both equally perfectly happy, and equal to her bridegroom. Although both parties speculate on their families' opinions as to who will be most fortunate in the alliance, Mr. Knightley insists on the importance of their "equal worth": "'I wish your father might be half as easily convinced as John will be, of our having every right that equal worth can give, to be happy together'" (465). And the narrator confirms this equality, saying of the union that "It was all right, all open, all equal. No sacrifice on any side worth the name. It was a union of the highest promise of felicity in itself" (468).

While such praise of hero and heroine is not uniquely epithalamic, the way that Austen emphasizes the place of their marriage in society and the potential for good in their strong ties to each other and to their families and community has a great deal to do with the tradition of the epithalamium. The Greek rhetorician Menander, for example, writes that the epithalamium should express the idea that "the ordering of the universe—air, stars, sea— took place because of Marriage: this god put an end to dispute and joined heaven and earth in concord and the rite of wedlock; whereupon all things were separated and took up their proper stations" (139). In her understanding of marriage as the establishment of peace and harmony—witness Harriet's prospects of "security, stability and improvement. . . . respectab[ility] and happ[iness]" (482)—Austen focuses on weddings as symbols and harbingers of mutual and communal benefit.

Mrs. Weston sees the potential for good in the marriage of Emma and Mr. Knightley: "she saw in it only increase of happiness to all" (467). She knows that Mr. Knightley's choice to remove to Hartfield is crucial to famil-ial harmony, and recognizes "How very few of those men in a rank of life to address Emma would have renounced their own home for Hartfield!" It seems to her "in every respect so proper, suitable, and unexceptionable a con-nection" (467), and, once Mr. Weston has spread the news through Jane and Miss Bates to Mrs. Cole, Mrs. Perry, and Mrs. Elton, it turns out, of course, that "In general, it was a very well approved match" (468). The community offers its blessing on the marriage, and peace and harmony seem assured. John Michael Neary notes that in *Jane Austen: Irony as Defense and Discovery* (1952), Marvin Mudrick "sees even the ultimate harmony established ritual-istically through marriage to be empty, ironic, beriddled"; in an examination of riddles and irony in *Emma*, Neary refutes Mudrick and concludes that Austen's "use of riddles points toward a more optimistic faith than this, a faith in marriage as a true symbol of at least potential harmony" (65).[1] Marriage in *Emma* represents the possibilities for harmony in both the private world and the social world, and even Mr. Woodhouse begins to reconcile himself to the idea of his daughter's marriage.

While the major subject of the epithalamium is usually the celebration of the wedding and of the present happiness of bride, bridegroom, family, and community, a potential problem of the genre is that it often neglects the ensuing marriage. Thus, although Spenser details the full twenty-four hours of his wedding day in his "Epithalamion," he does not talk at all about life after the celebrations. Sidney's "Song of the Shepherd Dicus at the Marriage of Thyrsis and Kala," from the *Arcadia* (1593), though not as pretty a wedding poem, is more worthy of praise as marriage poetry, because it deals realistically with the problems and possibilities of marriage rather than just the beauties of the wedding. If the wedding day is the climax, the marriage will necessarily be anticlimactic.[2]

All too often, Austen novels are thought of as simply romances with happy endings and weddings, and many of the film versions of the novels perpetuate, to varying degrees, this myth of pure romance. For example, how many people watching the 1995 A&E/BBC version of the ending of *Pride and Prejudice*, with its elaborate double wedding, lace, carriages, and kissing, remember easily and clearly that all Austen says of that wedding is this: "Happy for all her maternal feelings was the day on which Mrs. Bennet got rid of her two most deserving daughters" (385). The novels do end with marriages, but movies that invent a grand show of the wedding day miss the point that no amount of finery or celebration on the wedding day can make a marriage: what really matters is the harmony that develops and is established by two individuals before the wedding. It is the process and progress of love that are most significant, and while the religious and legal ceremony is necessary and important,[3] central to each of the novels is that process of development of character and discovery of love that leads to marriage, not the game of flirtation and financial calculation that leads merely to wedding. The latter is rightly left to the Lydias, Mrs. Bennets, and Mrs. Eltons of the world.

Quoting Milton's "L'Allegro," Mrs. Elton makes use of the conventional poetic language of wedding, saying that poor Mr. E despaired that the wedding could not come soon enough, and that he exclaimed that "'he was sure at this rate it would he May before Hymen's saffron robe would be put on for us'" (308). It is Mrs. Elton, not Austen, Emma, or Mr. Knightley, who is interested in the conventions of the wedding day. She likes "saffron robes" and lace and trimmings, as Miss Bates notes at the ball—"'dear Mrs. Elton, how elegant she looks!—Beautiful lace!'" (329)—despite her protestations to the contrary:

> "I have the greatest dislike to the idea of being over-trimmed—quite a horror of finery.... A bride, you know, must appear like a bride, but my natural taste is all for simplicity; a simple style of dress is so infinitely preferable to finery. But I am quite in the minority, I believe; few people seem to value simplicity of dress,—shew and finery are every thing. I have some notion of putting such a trimming as this to my white and silver poplin. Do you think it will look well?" (302)

Because *Emma*, like Austen's other novels, is about marriage as a lengthy process rather than about wedding as a single event, the actual material details of the wedding are relatively unimportant, and so the wedding between Emma and Mr. Knightley "was very much like other weddings, where the parties have no taste for finery or parade" (484).

Mrs. Elton notes the "deficiencies" of the wedding as compared to convention and to her own wedding day—"'Very little white satin, very few lace veils; a most pitiful business!—Selina would stare when she heard of it,'" but clearly Austen's focus is on the marriage rather than the wedding, as "the wishes, the hopes, the confidence, the predictions of the small band of true friends who witnessed the ceremony, were fully answered in the perfect happiness of the union" (484). Reversing the convention of detailing the trappings and finery and celebrations of the wedding day and choosing instead to emphasize the praiseworthy qualities of bride and bridegroom as they are valued by the community and as they represent a promise of future married happiness, stability, and peace, Austen follows the tradition of the epithalamium more along the lines of that practised by Sidney, rather than Spenser. Peter L. De Rose chronicles the progress of Emma's self-knowledge and the development of her relationship to Mr. Knightley, invoking Samuel Johnson's words to describe the marriage as "the most solemn league of perpetual friendship" (215). After Emma's romantic scene with Mr. Knightley "she was now in an exquisite flutter of happiness," but significantly, because her friendship with him is already so strong, she believes that this happiness "must still be greater when the flutter should have passed away" (434).

One of the most significant of the epithalamic conventions that appears at the end of the novel is the inclusion of the fescennine element. Although Austen's epithalamium so far has praised bride and bridegroom, their place in their families and their community, their prospects for future harmony, and wishes and blessings for happiness, and although the novel stresses the real importance of lasting mutual love and true union over the fleeting pleasures of the wedding day, in order to ensure that the marriage is peaceful the epithalamium must also banish evil. Fescennine verses included in marriage poetry are often bawdy and always represent an awareness of the potential dangers in marriage, sometimes sexual, sometimes political, sometimes simply any kind of threat to peace and security. The reason for including verses or passages on unpleasant topics in the midst of a wedding celebration is to recognize that the evils are there, and by recognizing them, the poet or narrator can banish them. In fairy-tales, this means inviting the bad fairies to the christening so that they won't feel left out and torment the child later on.

In *Emma*, the fescennine tradition appears in the character of Mr. Woodhouse's fears about housebreaking and poultry thieves: "Mrs. Weston's poultry-house was robbed one night of all her turkeys—evidently by the ingenuity of man. . . . Pilfering was *housebreaking* to Mr. Woodhouse's fears.—He was very uneasy; and but for the sense of his son-in-law's protection, would have been under wretched alarm every night of his life" (483–84). This passage is humorous, but it also serves the purpose of acknowledging that despite a perfect wedding, the future is not necessarily ideal for the hero and heroine. For one thing, they will have to continue to contend patiently with the fears of a difficult old man, and for another, there is still the very real possibility, despite Mr. Woodhouse's exaggerated response to this episode of theft, that the various evils of the larger world will impinge at some point on the peaceful, secluded universe of Hartfield and Donwell. Mr. Knightley will protect Mr. Woodhouse, Hartfield, and Emma—something that he can do all the better for having recognized that there are potential dangers. For the continued safety and harmony established by the marriage, it is important that the epithalamium admit the possibility of imperfections and evil and then banish them as far as possible.

Once evils are dispensed with, the marriage can proceed happily, and Austen does sum up the wedding and Mrs. Elton's objections to it quite neatly. George Whalley says, in fact, that the closing chapter of *Emma* "is one of the few places in all [Austen's] novels where I feel she is writing a little perfunctorily" (130). Yet at the same time he praises the ending of *Mansfield Park*—with its considerably more abrupt "I only entreat everybody to believe that exactly at the time when it was quite natural that it should be so, and not a week earlier, Edmund did cease to care about Miss Crawford, and became as anxious to marry Fanny, as Fanny herself could desire"—as "clos[ing] with . . . despatch, yet with something of the elegiac recognition of sheer necessity" (131). Whalley says that in *Emma* it is as if "for the author . . . all passion is spent." But I would argue that in ending with the brief description of the wedding of Emma and Mr. Knightley, Austen leaves possibilities open for their marriage. All has been agreed between them, and there is nothing more to be said. To see the chapter as a concise epithalamium about harmony rather than as a perfunctory summary of events is to appreciate the precision of Austen's language that Whalley has praised so highly, and the sense of the mutual love and passion that makes the dramatic action of the novel real and possible. The ending is not abrupt; the epithalamic celebration is not merely conventional, but innovative in its focus on marriage rather than wedding conventions, realistic in its inclusion of fescennine elements, and appropriately dramatic in that the ending fulfills the needs of the plot.

In Austen's exploration of the tension between romantic wedding and real marriage, she is at the height of her critical powers: although *Emma* deals with the events that lead to weddings, it is not simply a romantic story, because inherent in the development of love between Emma and Mr. Knightley is the recognition of real problems of life, character, behaviour, and marriage. And whereas in *Pride and Prejudice* Austen lightly dispenses with the weddings of Jane and Elizabeth, leaving this business to superficial characters only, in *Emma* she celebrates the real bond of attachment and marriage throughout the novel and in its last paragraph, while still allowing Mrs. Elton dominion over the lace and satin. In this balance lies true criticism: it is criticism that does not merely dismiss and disdain the superficial, but that at the same time confidently celebrates the real and offers praise for what is good.

In *Emma* Austen, consciously or not, makes use generally of some of the generic conventions of the epithalamium, yet it is not so much the presence of conventions that makes the ending an epithalamium, and Austen a poet, as the absence of the superfluous trappings of wedding. Once Mr. Woodhouse has commanded evil to be banished, the lace-free marriage can prosper. Austen participates in the tradition of the poetry of marriage rather than the poetry of wedding, as the relationship between Emma and Mr. Knightley is worked out throughout the novel, from the moment Emma first says, "'We always say what we like to one another'" (10). The ending is not perfunctory, but the appropriate culmination of a process in which bride and bridegroom come to know each other. The whole novel is an epithalamium in that it explores a relationship that will eventually be a harmonious marriage between equals, and thus the concise ending is more central to the tradition of the epithalamium than any description of the elaborate wedding (for Mrs. Elton's benefit) or even any more detailed ending (for Whalley's) could ever be. The ending of *Emma* includes many of the conventions of the epithalamium, and in focussing on the future promise of marriage rather than on the wedding day, Austen participates in the best tradition of the poetry not of wedding, but of marriage.[4]

Notes

1. Although Neary's dissertation is entitled "Stories of Marriage: The Epithalamial Imaginations of Jane Austen, Charles Dickens, and James Joyce," he does not discuss the conventions of the epithalamium as they relate to the novels, but instead uses the term generally to refer to the subject of marriage.

2. In the same way, if the proposal scene is the real climax of the novel, the marriage may be seen as anti-climax. For discussions of whether or not Austen's proposal scenes are anti-climax, see Janis P. Stout, "Jane Austen's Proposal Scenes and the Limitations of Language," *Studies in the Novel* 14.4 (1982): 316–26; Kathleen Lundeen, "A Modest Proposal? Paradise Found in Jane Austen's Betrothal Scenes," *Review of English Studies* 41.161 (1990): 65–75; T. Mildred Wherritt, "For Better or for Worse: Marriage Proposals in Jane Austen's Novels," *Midwest Quarterly* 17 (1976): 229–44.

3. Marianne Dashwood's misguided reliance on the emotional bond alone serves to demonstrate the significance of the official ceremony: she says of Willoughby that "I felt myself to be as solemnly engaged to him, as if the strictest legal covenant had bound us to each other."

4. My thanks are due to the Killam Trust and the Social Sciences and Humanities Research Council of Canada for supporting this research.

Works Cited

Austen, Jane. *Emma*. Ed. R. W. Chapman. 3rd ed. London: Oxford UP, 1932.

———. *Pride and Prejudice*. Ed. R W. Chapman. 3rd ed. London: Oxford UP, 1932.

———. *Sense and Sensibility*. Ed. R. W. Chapman. 3rd ed. London: Oxford UP, 1932.

De Rose, Peter L. "Marriage and Self-Knowledge in *Emma* and *Pride and Prejudice*." *Renascence* 30 (1978): 199–216.

Neary, John Michael. "Stories of Marriage: The Epithalamial Imaginations of Jane Austen, Charles Dickens, and James Joyce." *DAI* 42.9 (1982): 4009A.

Russell, D. A., and N. G. Wilson, eds. *Menander Rhetor*. Oxford: Clarendon, 1981.

Tufte, Virginia. *The Poetry of Marriage: The Epithalamium in Europe and Its Development in England*. Los Angeles: Tinnon-Brown, 1970.

Whalley, George. "Jane Austen: Poet." *Jane Austen's Achievement*. Ed. Juliet McMaster. London: Macmillan; New York: Harper, 1976. 106–33.

ISOBEL GRUNDY

Why Do They Talk So Much?
How Can We Stand It?

Let us first take a quick look at excessive talkers in literature before Jane Austen. It seems that this tradition, like so many, began in English with Shakespeare: in, particularly, *Romeo and Juliet*. The founder of this tradition is not Mercutio or even Romeo before he meets Juliet, though the flow of language in these two young men (a fashion in their day) can well be played as excessive. There is nothing modish in the gabbiness of Juliet's nurse. We first meet her when Juliet's mother, Lady Capulet, arrives on stage to break it to Juliet that her parents have a husband picked out. She intends to talk to her daughter privately, but Nurse just refuses to leave, and Lady Capulet, knowing when she's beaten, lets her stay. Lady Capulet is then totally upstaged. Her weighty secret has to wait while Nurse delivers herself of a thirty-two-line speech of reminiscence about Juliet as a little girl. When Lady Capulet can get a word in edgeways she says, "Enough of this; I pray thee hold thy peace"—and Nurse spends another eight lines repeating her punch-line (I.iii.51–59). This is just the beginning. At later tense moments in the action, both Romeo and Juliet have to wait for her torrent of language to subside before they can get some absolutely crucial piece of information out of her.

In Shakespeare this is wonderful. It provides that famous comic relief; it keeps up suspense; it grounds the high-flown passion of the young lovers

From *The Talk in Jane Austen*, edited by Bruce Stovel and Lynn Weinlos Gregg, pp. 41–56. © 2002 by the University of Alberta Press.

in Nurse's earthiness and total lack of moral scruples—and it obliquely questions the rigid social hierarchy that is meant to prevail in Verona. Servants—like women and children—are supposed to be seen and not heard. The infringement of propriety helps to make Nurse's gabbiness both funny and attractive.

The joke about servants' excessive talk was used by Goldsmith in *She Stoops to Conquer* and hinted at by Horace Walpole in *The Castle of Otranto* (33–36). It was picked up enthusiastically by later novelists, especially gothic novelists. Even Ann Radcliffe has a touch of it. The principle seems to be that servants will run on excessively and irrelevantly, holding up the action, when things are tense and haste is vital. Their loquacity is not merely insubordinate (as with Nurse), but also a clear sign of their intellectual inferiority (not like Nurse, who is nobody's fool). The talk of these later servants is characterized firstly by a mass of trivial circumstantial detail and secondly by the wildest exaggeration. These talkers have no sense of proportion, no power of prioritizing, no recognition of what's important (except that they think—wrongly—that they are themselves important). This all suggests that the authors of these novels are social conservatives: obliquely, they convey approval of the socially imposed silence of servants, since when servants are allowed to talk the results are so regrettable.

The over-talkative servant, like so many stock motifs, became grist for Jane Austen to pick up and transform. John Thorpe and Miss Bates are related to all those fictional long-winded servants, but the relationship is not one of simple family resemblance or simple contrast. Austen's juvenilia show her to have been deeply delighted both by irrelevance and by exaggeration, not when those qualities are comfortably confined to the lower classes but when they are rampant among her own class equals.

The talking-servant tradition is a reason for excluding from this essay Mr. Collins, whose talk has been so well anatomized by Juliet McMaster.[1] Mr. Collins is certainly interminable, but his style of talk does not derive from Juliet's Nurse. Its meaning is impeded, not by circumstantial detail or exaggeration, but by an overabundance of elaborate syntax. It is clergy talk, satirizing the specialized discourse of the pulpit. Though Mr. Collins is to some extent socially disadvantaged, as his social grovelling demonstrates, it is not to his social superiors that he lets himself go in loquacity, but to unprivileged female audiences. He speaks to those below him from his authority as a clergyman. His long-windedness is in no way subversive.

Matters are obviously quite different with Miss Bates, and I believe they are different too with John Thorpe. Miss Bates is the heart of this essay, but John Thorpe provides a useful approach to it. In relation to Catherine Morland, he has the privilege of gender: his talkativeness is contrasted with that of Henry Tilney. Both claim Catherine's ear because they are male and she is female. But although Thorpe is a university student, he is as close, socially speaking, to Miss Bates as to Henry Tilney. Despite his implicit claims of having unlimited funds, his mother is "a widow, and not a very rich one" (*NA* 34), just like Miss Bates's mother. I believe that John Thorpe, like Miss Bates but from a different angle, may be designed as a comment on the stereotyped, novelistic, over-talkative servant.

Thorpe is introduced by his friend James Morland as "a little of a rattle" (50). Bingley in *Pride and Prejudice* is a rattle, too, but Jane Austen does not subject her readers to his rattling. Nor does she subject them to Thorpe's monologues in the way she does with those of Miss Bates. It is Catherine who gets bored to tears by John Thorpe, not the reader. And his boring talk to Catherine is insignificant, while it is other talk of his, which the reader never hears, that significantly shapes the plot.

Austen's depiction of John Thorpe is positively economical. We learn all the essential characteristics of his talk in Chapter 7, when Catherine, who has only just met him, is thoroughly supplied with information about his horse and gig. He shares with all these servants an addiction to unnecessary detail: the story of his gig purchase includes the exact spot where it took place (which means nothing to Catherine, who has not been to Oxford), the character of the vendor, exactly what was said on each side including the swear words, and the exact price. The last is presented as a punch-line, as if it is deeply significant; but then it turns out to be a boringly medium price, of no significance whatever. In this chapter, Thorpe establishes his descent from the gothic servant tradition, with irrelevant, compulsive detail and desperate exaggeration. This is the occasion on which he says of his horse, "Only see how he moves; that horse *cannot* go less than ten miles an hour: tie his legs and he will get on" (46).[2]

In conventional fiction, these characteristics—irrelevance, exaggeration, and self-centredness—distinguish the chatty servants from the sensitive, refined characters on whom the story centres. Middle- or upper-class persons do not talk like that; nor do they ever take a servant's exaggerations seriously. But in *Northanger Abbey* these qualities are not confined to the lower orders. Thorpe, who embodies them, is a person of some status and class pretension, and an individual with real status; no less a person than General Tilney takes him seriously. So does Catherine. She learns quite quickly not to take his word about social trivia, but finds it much harder to apply this lesson to more serious subjects.

After that first monologue, Austen takes to protecting her readers. In the next chapter John Thorpe is given more reported than direct speech. This is where he keeps engaging Catherine to dance and then not dancing at all, leaving her prohibited by social etiquette from dancing with anyone else, specifically with Henry Tilney. When he does return to Catherine, we hear that she is unconsoled by "the particulars which he entered into while they were standing up, of the horses and dogs of the friend whom he had just left, and of a proposed exchange of terriers between them" (55). In Chapter 9, on the drive up Claverton Down, we get some choice snippets of his conversational style: "Old Allen is as rich as a Jew—is not he?" (63) and "There is not the hundredth part of the wine consumed in this kingdom, that there ought to be" (64). But we get more summary than samples: "of horses which he had bought for a trifle and sold for incredible sums; of racing matches, in which his judgment had infallibly foretold the winner; of shooting parties, in which he had killed more birds . . . than all his companions together" (66) and so on. And we get more summary than précis: "his rapidity of expression" (64), "idle assertions and impudent falsehoods" (65), "the effusions of his endless conceit" (66). We are allowed to see through John Thorpe without having to hear him out.

And so we as readers are allowed, or encouraged, to be surprised at the way General Tilney falls for Thorpe's inconsequentiality and exaggeration. Through John Thorpe, and by presenting him through authorial summary, Austen restores the potential humour in this kind of excessive talk. She also makes the point that it can have serious consequences when such talk is not safely confined to servants but becomes dangerously prevalent among middle-class idiots who expect to be listened to.

Miss Bates is equally irrelevant, equally excessive, but not in the same way exaggerated or self-centred. Talking too much is virtually her defining characteristic. The narrator sums her up at the outset as "a great talker upon little matters . . . full of trivial communications [like John Thorpe] and *harmless* gossip [unlike him]" (*E* 21; emphasis added). But the narrator, who stepped forward with so many similar summaries in *Northanger Abbey* (who, as it were, talked a great deal in that novel), now steps back, or falls almost silent, leaving Miss Bates to speak for herself. Her first prodigious feat of talking is performed the first time that, as readers, we actually meet her. Six pages of print (*E* 156–62) are needed "to usher in" (156) the reading of a letter from Jane Fairfax: six pages largely devoted to Miss Bates's talk, with a bare minimum of narration and only a sentence or two from Emma.

This is a virtuoso performance, on Austen's part as well as that of her creation, in which all the inimitable characteristics of Miss Bates's talking style are not told but shown. Miss Bates has so little management of suspense or surprise that her first move in ushering in Jane's letter is to relate exactly how Mrs. Cole had thought there would not be a letter yet, and how surprised she had been to hear that there was one. She loses the letter and explains at great length how it was that she came to lose it, and how it came to be where it actually was all the time (157). Angling for a compliment to Jane's beautifully legible handwriting, she ties herself in knots over the deterioration of her mother's eyesight, coupled with a fervent Pangloss-like assertion that her eyesight is after all excellent *for her age* (157–58). And of course the brevity of Jane's letter is taken to need elaborate apology (157). Although almost nothing Miss Bates says is to the point, not a scrap of it is wasted. Every word goes towards proving some point of Jane Austen's.

Miss Bates begins as Austen meant her to go on. Later, her arrival with Mrs. Weston is the arrival of "one voice and two ladies" (235). She herself confesses only half apologetically to being "rather a talker" (346). Her constant talking becomes a running joke, like Mr. Woodhouse's valetudinarianism. She asks, "What was I talking of?", and Emma wonders "On what, of all the medley, she would fix" (237). Miss Bates leaves sentences unfinished. She twice says Mr. Knightley is, or would be, "so very" (238, 239): not very anything, just so very—a joke inspired by the popular rhetorical claim that a hero or heroine's charms defy the reach of language. She never fails to tell one person what she has said to another, no matter how vacuous the comment. This, too, she leaves unfinished: "I said to my mother, 'Upon my word, ma'am'" (322). Full stop. Having nothing to say is no deterrent to her: still, the other characters are pursued by "the sounds of her desultory good-will" (239), telling them to mind the step. (This is the woman who also warns of two steps when there is in fact only one [329].)

Emma finds Miss Bates even more boring than Catherine found John Thorpe. It is Emma herself, not the narrator, who both complains and jokes about this subject. She makes a joke of it not once but twice, though one occasion has been much more noticed in criticism than the other. In this novel Austen no longer protects her readers from the boring talk, as she did in *Northanger Abbey*, and it is worth considering why, if Miss Bates really is so boring, Austen makes it compulsory to listen to her for pages at a time.

A generation or two ago the stock question about this issue was: How does Jane Austen keep us interested in pages of Miss Bates, whereas in life we would be shifting in our seats like Emma, looking for a chance to escape? Because I no longer believe Miss Bates to be simply boring, I think this was the wrong question. Whole chapters might be too much, but whole pages are just right. Austen produces Miss Bates's talk through the filter of her own artistry: she achieves the paradox of apparently artless mimesis, shepherding our reactions in the direction she chooses.

Plenty of other issues arise about Miss Bates, as well as the question of her excessive talk: the matter of her moral goodness, her class position, her structural relation to the character of Emma. In each of these her loquacity is vital to her presentation.

The narrator makes much of Miss Bates's goodness, her courage in adversity, her happiness: "her own universal good-will and contented temper . . . The simplicity and cheerfulness of her nature, her contented and grateful spirit . . . a mine of felicity to herself" (21). This sounds like the conduct-book ideal, yet Miss Bates's constant talking is the very reverse of what conduct books recommend. Again, awareness of the talking-servant tradition might seem to lower Miss Bates's class position. Yet the plot of the novel insists on the parallel—neither a simple likeness nor quite a simple contrast—between her and Emma. Emma is "handsome, clever, and rich" (5); Miss Bates is "neither young, handsome, rich, nor married" (21). (Austen's silence about her lack of cleverness is a joke that becomes apparent only on a second reading.) Emma dislikes Jane Fairfax; Miss Bates dotes on her. When Emma says she could happily live unmarried, Harriet says fearfully, "But then, to be an old maid at last, like Miss Bates!" (84).

On the other side of the argument, Emma is never tedious, but says just what she ought, while Miss Bates is always tedious and says much more than she ought. These characters, however, are nothing so simple as opposites. Emma is like Miss Bates in having a "happy disposition" (57), though hers has not been tried and tested. The older woman's happiness is a paradox. On the one hand it bears out a favourite moral of contemporary fiction writers and conduct writers (indeed, of any writer addressing a female or largely female audience): that the good are always happy, indeed that nobody but the good can be happy. Austen, therefore, is calling the conventional moralists' bluff. Miss Bates's brand of goodness is not a recipe for happiness that they could afford to accept. Miss Bates as a model to follow would compromise the reliance of conventional moralists on the promised reward of happiness. Conduct books exist to guide young ladies to marriage and material comfort, not to entertain the possibility of developing into a Miss Bates.

I believe Austen is denying the morality of offering goodness as the high road to happiness, exposing the true conduct-literature lesson as a lesson in how to be a heroine. For this it is not enough to be handsome, clever, and—at least at the end of the story—rich. It is also necessary to be interesting to the reader, to have potential for change and development, which also implies potential for being unhappy. Austen requires her heroines to be teachable, but not in the manner of conduct literature. In such literature, a teachable woman is "docile." Against the simple model of education as pouring good teaching into a passive receptacle, Austen sets up an interactive model, depending on the agency of the pupil at least as much as that of the teacher. That is the point of this digression: Miss Bates's loquacity signifies that she does not and cannot learn. She never listens (being too busy putting out sound that no one is expected to listen to), while Emma learns, over the course of the action, to listen well.

Another point of relationship between Emma and Miss Bates is the unmarried status they share. Miss Bates, with her moral virtue, her happiness, and her talk, is designed as an intervention into another social debate often found in novels: the nature of the old maid. Is or is not a typical old maid sour, narrow, embittered, altogether a proof of the incompleteness of the female without the male? A key text here, though no longer new at the date of *Emma*, is William Hayley's *Essay on Old Maids* (1785). (Hayley dedicated his book, with amazing assurance, to Elizabeth Carter, whom he presents as the exception to a norm entirely lacking in goodness or happiness.) Many women writers before and after Hayley represented an opposite viewpoint, and a few of them were probably well known to Austen.[3] Some women novelists in pursuit of this ideological point allowed the courtship of their heroines to be upstaged by some other, more marginal but more unusual, unmarried female character.[4] It is not Austen's way to make ideological assertions; she offers possibilities and jokes. Nevertheless, Miss Bates's happiness is designed partly in support of the anti-William Hayley, pro-old maid side of the argument.[5]

This may sound like a paradox, since Austen is also holding up Miss Bates as a specimen for the reader's amusement. It is important in this context that Miss Bates is not presented in contrast with other, quieter characters. In *Emma* almost all the characters talk a lot, and many of them too much. Emma exchanges long speeches with almost all her friends and acquaintances. Harriet, when we first meet her, is having her "talkativeness" "encouraged" by Emma (27); she pours out desultory detail with a "youthful simplicity" (27) which sounds very like Miss Bates: "He had a very fine flock; and . . . he had been bid more for his wool than any body in the country. . . . Mrs. Martin was so very kind as to send Mrs. Goddard a beautiful goose: the finest goose Mrs. Goddard had ever seen. Mrs. Goddard had dressed it on a Sunday, and asked all the three teachers, Miss Nash, and Miss Prince, and Miss Richardson, to sup with her" (28–29). Talk in this style—and even more that of Mr. Woodhouse on the topic of the Hartfield pork (172)—has something in common with that of John Thorpe, who constantly aggrandizes himself by claiming to have the best of everything. But Mr. Woodhouse is making a present of his superior pork, and Harriet is aggrandizing the Martin family, not herself (even though at one remove this is a kind of self-aggrandizing). Austen seems to have given up guiding her readers' responses and to be leaving their judgements entirely free. Talk is therefore not to be considered for its quantity alone.

Frank Churchill shares in the general wordiness of Highbury; he irritates Mr. Knightley by the length of his final letter as well as by its contents. He even manages to make a single word, "blunder," excessive. Mr. Elton, hearing, like Mr. Collins, the stamp of his profession, has "a sort of parade in his speeches which was very apt to incline [Emma] to laugh" (82). Mrs. Elton at her first introduction seems a talker ready to rival Miss Bates, and her manner of handling her leitmotif, the barouche-landau, recalls John Thorpe and his gig (274). Jane Austen chooses to represent Mrs. Elton's talk by its effect on others. Once, when in full flow, "She was stopped by a slight fit of coughing, . . . Mr. Weston instantly seized the opportunity of going on" (308). Another time Mr. Knightley "seemed to be trying not to smile; and succeeded without difficulty, upon Mrs. Elton's beginning to talk to him" (312).

The general level of public talk at Highbury is summed up at the Coles' dinner party: "a few clever things said, a few downright silly, but by much the larger proportion neither the one nor the other—nothing worse than every day remarks, dull repetitions, old news, and heavy jokes" (219). The private talk we know to be different from this, for by this stage in the novel we have read pages and pages of dialogue, often sparkling or at least intelligent, and when silly, generally redeemed either by the imagination of Emma or by the goodwill of Harriet or Mr. Woodhouse—or Miss Bates.

Miss Bates is flanked by her mother and by Jane Fairfax, probably the two quietest characters in the novel. Yet her loquacity is contrasted less with their silence than with the different loquacities of other people. Sometimes, indeed, the contrast is pointed. Take Mrs. Elton's celebrated soliloquy at the strawberry-picking, beginning with "The best fruit in England—every body's favourite—always wholesome.—These the finest beds and finest sorts" and ending with "—only objection to gathering strawberries the stooping—glaring sun—tired to death—could bear it no longer—must go and sit in the shade" (358–59). This monologue is clearly designed to contrast with two much longer soliloquies delivered earlier, just a few pages apart, by Miss Bates at a comparable social gathering: the ball (322–23, 328–30). Whereas Mrs. Elton's speech runs downhill from rhapsody into disillusion, both of Miss Bates's soliloquies sustain their enjoyment. It takes the arrival of tea the first time, and food the second time, to shut her up. Her first speech begins "So very obliging of you!—No rain at all. Nothing to signify. I do not care for myself. . . . Well! This is brilliant indeed!—This is admirable!" and ends with the exclamation "Everything so good!" (322–23). Of course Miss Bates's capacity to sustain her happiness, or enjoyment, despite rain is contrasted with Mrs. Elton's reaction to sun, and it is to be counted as moral virtue. Her talk is also a constant validation of others, concern for others, and applause for others' concern for her. Miss Bates's talk weaves a web of interdependence, of reciprocity, the exchange of the trivial pleasures of gossip. When she hears the news of Mr. Elton's marriage, she rushes first to pass the story on to the Woodhouses, then back to visit with Mrs. Cole, who had told the news to her in a note (172–73, 176). She has to give thanks for the gift of news; she has to pass it on; talk is both her only wealth and her medium of exchange.

So the sheer excess is tied up with many other characteristics: those of irrelevance, of tedium, of gossip, of dailiness, of exchange and reciprocation. Although Emma's famous snub at Box Hill turns on the issue of tedium, I believe some of the other issues are more important. They are mostly issues raised in Miss Bates's very first speech, which concerns Jane Fairfax's letter, nineteen chapters into the novel. Ronald Blythe's introduction to the Penguin edition of the novel links her late entrance with the lapse of the seasons: winter comes first in *Emma*; Miss Bates's "starling chatter" heralds the spring (23). There is naturalistic observation in this: Mrs. and Miss Bates's social lives would be sharply curtailed in winter, which also restricts general social life in Highbury and gives Emma an excuse for not visiting them. But there is more to this than naturalism, for Miss Bates has another season of silence: she stops talking well before the novel's close, a silencing that I will discuss shortly.

Emma's famous Box Hill snub turns on both tedium and excess. Perhaps no scene is better known. Frank Churchill sets up his parlour game: everyone is to contribute to the conversation either one very clever thing or two things moderately clever or three things very dull indeed. Churchill here echoes the narrator describing the talk at the Coles' dinner party. Miss Bates cheerfully offers to be dull, and Emma insists on her excess as well as dullness, doubting that Miss Bates can limit herself to three dull things (370). Here the novel seems to pause: this is one of the rare moments when the silence of other people is commented on. No reader can miss the point that Emma is being unkind, and in her author's moral world that means she is being set up for rebuke and repentance. Yet I believe every first-time reader of this passage enters happily, shamelessly into Emma's joke, into her feeling of superiority (she surely feels she is saying one very clever thing), into her scoring off Miss Bates. But then Austen sharply divides herself from the Emma we have been laughing with. The moment is not allowed to pass. When Miss Bates gets the point, she registers shock and hurt: "I will try to hold my tongue. I must make myself very disagreeable, or she would not have said such a thing to an old friend" (373). And Mr. Knightley follows this up with his fierce private sentencing of Emma (374–75).

This scene is, of course, beautifully contextualized, Frank is out to make trouble; he flirts with Emma because he is beginning to quarrel seriously with Jane, Emma is drunk on flirtation and flattery, and also wound up to competitiveness by Mrs. Elton. Mr. Knightley is finding an unacknowledged outlet for suppressed jealousy. But what of Miss Bates? Is it really in character for her to be so wounded? Nowhere else in the novel do we see her behaving at all like this, but then nowhere else is she similarly provoked.

It might be possible to argue that Austen is manipulating Miss Bates's character in the interests of the plot because Emma's superiority must be punctured. Or it might be argued that in this scene Miss Bates reveals unexpected hidden depths: a capacity for unhappiness, a concern not for someone else but for her own self-esteem.

To anybody reading Miss Bates as solely a comic butt, this moment would be out of character, indeed at odds with Austen's agenda for her. In any reading of her, it is an uncharacteristic moment. Other clues to her sensitivity, such as her phrase "if any thing was to happen" (160), which must refer to the likelihood that her mother has not long to live, are clues indeed, but are half-hidden: this moment is writ large.[6] But at each of these sensitive moments, it is Miss Bates's *succinctness* that signals an abnormal situation, a shift to a different and more inward register. Again Emma and Miss Bates are obliquely linked: this crucial moment for Emma is also, if anyone has attention to spare for it, a crucial moment for Miss Bates. It offers a rare clue to motivation and character construction: a reason for Miss Bates to talk so much is that it serves to protect her from the questions, or the sneers, of others.

An unprepared reader of the Box Hill scene is likely to side with Emma and so, as it were, to share her blame. Her other witticism about Miss Bates's conversation (made out of Miss Bates's hearing) is permitted to be funny without reproof. Here Emma is talking to the wonderfully non-judgemental Mrs. Weston: in this joke she mimics Miss Bates's talk. Whereas on Box Hill Emma openly tells Miss Bates that she is both dull and prolix, she here (before the Box Hill scene happens) exhibits Miss Bates to her audience of one as clownishly trivial and irrelevant: "and, indeed, she must thankfully say that their petticoats were all very strong" (225). This comment is ribald and unlady-like if not actually improper; at the same time it is clever and wickedly perceptive, and it hurts nobody.

Given a novel so closely concerned with social pressures, it would be naive to believe that this last remark shows the real Emma, while Box Hill shows an Emma distorted by stress. But it is fair to contrast the way Emma talks before an intimate friend with the way she talks before a part-hostile audience, and perhaps also to suggest that her method on Box Hill, of telling her audience what to think, resembles Austen's method with John Thorpe, while her method with Mrs. Weston resembles Austen's method with Miss Bates. In building Miss Bates's character through a display of her talk, Austen parallels Emma's mimicry of Miss Bates. She excels in detail, verisimilitude, and insight, while Emma, rather like Austen's juvenile writing self, excels in panache, fantasy, and deliberate outrageousness.

In view of the common ground cautiously sketched between Emma and Miss Bates, we may also ask how much common ground Austen envisaged between Miss Bates and herself. The parallel between Miss Bates's discourse and that of Emma has not gone unnoticed. But the discourse of trivia (drawing detail from one's own little corner of the world, filling up emptiness, enmeshing people in tiny connections) was used by Austen herself, not in fiction but in letters.[7] In Miss Bates this tendency is artless; in Austen's letters it is a technique that deliberately ignores both scale and plot. It is a validation of that common, ordinary, unadorned life that is the water in which Miss Bates swims, and which novelists as a class, but Austen in particular, have taken as their bailiwick.

Austen brings Emma into somewhat uneasy relation with such ordinariness in the passage—another famous one—in which Emma whiles away the time, as Harriet dithers over her shopping, by looking out of the shop door. The greatest event she might hope for would be "Mr. Cole's carriage horses returning from exercise, or a stray letter-boy on an obstinate mule"; more likely would be the butcher making deliveries, an old woman shopping, "two curs quarrelling over a dirty bone, and a string of dawdling children round the baker's little bow-window eyeing the gingerbread. . . . A mind lively and at ease, can do with seeing nothing, and can see nothing that does not answer" (233).

Critics have generally taken this moment as Austen's endorsement of the quotidian. But is this a moment (or, indeed, a novel) concerned with endorsement? Does the author in this passage take it upon herself to tell her readers that a lively mind at ease with itself can fill up the vacancies of life with trivia? Or is this indirect speech in which Emma tells herself these things? If these are Emma's aphorisms then they lie as open and vulnerable to criticism as do her projected reading lists elsewhere (37) and her conviction that she has plenty of resources and needs no stimulus from the outside (85). Are we really to imbibe from Emma the message that dailiness is enough?

I do not believe that Emma finds it enough. It is Miss Bates who does. This is Miss Bates's success, the key to her happiness, the thing that makes her mockable yet not pitiable, the thing, perhaps, that links her with her creator. The dogs with their bones, the children without their longed-for gingerbread, are not so trivial as Harriet's ridiculous love-tokens from Mr. Elton (338–40). They are that "every thing" which Frank Churchill believes to be readily available in female correspondence (261), and which some readers have complained of finding too much of in Austen's letters. Emma, as the heroine, can look through a door at these things and know that she moves among significant choices and important discoveries, as Miss Bates does not.

But Austen, who stands with Miss Bates, also stands with her heroine. A view from a shop door can make a letter but not a novel. In teasing Miss Bates, though not in snubbing her, Emma is doing what her creator herself has done. And indeed Austen goes further. She does what none of her characters can do and silences Miss Bates. In the bustle of closure, it is easy not to notice the full extent of her silencing. We are not allowed to hear a word from her on the match between Emma and Mr. Knightley; as if she were John Thorpe, her response is reported but not recorded. In fact all that is reported is her place in the grapevine that relays the news: the lovers tell the Westons, as a secret; Mr. Weston tells his almost-daughter-in-law, Jane, "and Miss Bates being present, it passed, of course, to Mrs. Cole, Mrs. Perry, and Mrs. Elton, immediately afterwards" (468). Miss Bates's voice is unheard.

That is not all. Miss Bates has already been stifled in her attempts to tell Emma (and through Emma the reader) about Jane's engagement to Frank. Emma "could not help being diverted by the perplexity of [Miss Bates's] first answer to herself, resulting, she supposed, from doubt of what might be said, and impatience to say every thing" (455). And Miss Bates actually keeps the secret: "Thank you, dear Miss Woodhouse, you are all kindness.—It is impossible to say—Yes, indeed, I quite understand—dearest Jane's prospects—that is, I do not mean—But she is charmingly recovered.—How is Mr. Woodhouse? . . . Charming young man!—that is—so very friendly; I mean good Mr. Perry!" (455). In these broken phrases I calculate that the truth reaches the tip of Miss Bates's tongue four or five times and is bitten back every time. Miss Bates struggles heroically and successfully not to behave like John Thorpe, not to let out other people's secrets—and when it is Jane's secret, not Emma's, she actually succeeds. So within the covers of the novel she never gets to comment on either marriage.

Yet in a sense this silencing is only temporary. Miss Bates has to be quieted so that the happy ending can take place: Austen would never allow her to upstage the heroine, as certain other novelists have with their ideologically polemical single women. But Miss Bates cannot be truly silenced. Though she says nothing about these happy weddings, her earlier monologues remain in the novel, available for rereading; and she is never reproved (as Emma is) for talking too much or inappropriately. Her late silencing may even be regarded as a means of leaving the way clear for the activity critics call "writing beyond the ending," but which is actually something that happens more frequently in talk than in writing.[8] The Austen family did it by letter, but they presumably did it with equal gusto and at greater length in talk. Readers are free to read the silencing of Miss Bates as an invitation for her to talk beyond her ending: an invitation to follow in Emma's footsteps and conjure up Miss Bates's remarks, not about petticoats, but about happy endings. Austen has made us share in her put-down of Emma for mocking Miss Bates to her face. She has also allowed us to share in a different mockery, the mockery of comic imitation, not description: mockery without contempt, or reproof, or pity, but expressive of the love of the intelligent, amused, and privileged listener for the lowly, irrepressible, excessive talker.

NOTES

1. See "Talking about Talk in *Pride and Prejudice*" 87.

2. Isabella is just like her brother, waiting "these ten ages at least" for Catherine, who is not really late at all (39).

3. They included the labouring-class Mary Collier a couple of generations back, Elizabeth Hamilton in an unpublished poem, several novelists, and Elizabeth Carter herself in letters.

4. See, for example, Jane Harvey, *Memoirs of an Author* (1812); Elizabeth Benger, *The Heart and the Fancy, or Valsimore, a Tale* (1813).

5. I also wonder if Miss Bates's happiness conceals a less public joke, an in-joke. Samuel Johnson is on record as frequently maintaining that people in general are not happy. He once confessed himself much irritated by a certain lady's claim to be happy—although, as he unkindly put it, she had neither money nor youth nor brains. If she could suppose herself happy, he seemed to suggest, no sensible person would wish to emulate her. You're wrong, says Jane Austen, look, here is a woman who is happy without any of those things. Despise her at your peril!

6. When I delivered this essay at the Jasper JASNA conference, a member of the audience reminded me afterwards of this vital clue. I am grateful.

7. Carol Houlihan Flynn writes well about this in her essay "The Letters."

8. See, especially, Rachel Blau DuPlessis's *Writing Beyond the Ending: Narrative Strategies of Twentieth-Century Women Writers*.

JOHN WILTSHIRE

Comfort, Health and Creativity:
A Reading of Emma

One of the chief challenges in teaching *Emma*, I've found, as with all
Jane Austen's novels, is to get students to move on from talking about characters and about the romance plot and to understand something of the novel's structure and its status as a work of art. This is all the more important
in the wake of the recent films, which, for very good reasons, replace Jane
Austen's artistic purposes and designs by their own, and almost inevitably
give a greater prominence to sexuality and romance than do the novels. In
the past there have been many attempts to read *Emma* by focusing on such
moral or pedagogical matters as the 'education' or 'humiliation' of Emma's
imagination or (more recently) on Emma's relation to the various manifestations of patriarchal society. In this chapter I suggest an approach that picks
up a relatively undernoticed preoccupation of the text, the quotidian but also
salient notion of 'comfort', and seek through this to call attention to what I
believe is a vital aspect of the novel's underlying conceptual, or rather emotional and ethical structure.

A way of beginning discussion of *Emma*, especially with students who
have read other Austen novels, but also with those who are studying this as an
example of her work for the first time, is to call attention to its densely populated textual space. One distinctive feature of *Emma* is the way it embeds its
action so convincingly within a small, circumscribed, but nevertheless active

From *Jane Austen: Introductions and Interventions*, pp. 95–107, 128. © 2003, 2006 by John
Wiltshire.

and convincingly detailed 'Highbury world'. This is achieved by numerous means, but one of the most effective is the passing mention—as if they were already known to the reader—of a number of figures who never actually make an appearance in the novel. The effect of this apparently casual citation of the names of Mrs Goddard, the Coles and William Larkins, among others, is to persuade the reader that he or she already knows them, and to create a narrator who is a denizen of the world she reports so familiarly upon. One of these figures, the notice of whom serves to populate Highbury and to thicken its description is the apothecary or the local doctor.

Mr Perry is in fact mentioned in *Emma* every twenty or so pages, in one connection or other, either through Mr Woodhouse's conversation, or seen passing through the town, or through reports of his medical opinion. His presence is more than incidental to the novel, however. Of course a small town would have its local doctor, just as it would have its local school, and local shopkeepers—many of whom are named, and even briefly characterised in *Emma*—the obsequious Mrs Ford, at the draper's shop, Mrs Wallis the baker's wife, who can sometimes give a rude answer (236–7). But (one might ask) isn't Mr Perry more important, more central to the novel's main interests than these figures, as his close relation (perhaps a friendship) with Emma's father suggests? Perry, a very active figure, often glimpsed on the road, always coming back from somewhere or other, is a familiar reference for the citizens of Highbury, but he's equally important as a pointer to some of the novel's leading interests. His very activity, which is also movement up the social scale, forms a telling contrast with the genteel inertia of his principal patient in the place, Mr Woodhouse.

The threading of Mr Perry through the narrative might lead one to think about Austen's interest in health in this novel. Serious illness is rare in *Emma* (the distant Mrs Churchill's medical emergencies are treated with suspicion) and Highbury's most dramatic bodily event—Mrs Weston's pregnancy and the birth of little Anna—occurs with only the briefest of facetious mentions. But minor ailments, and imagined illnesses, coughs, colds, biliousness, fever, fainting fits, a putrid sore throat, are common occurrences in the novel, and these are matters of considerable interest to the community Jane Austen depicts. In fact one might say that talk about health is the idiolect—the characteristic mode of human exchange—in Highbury. People fuss over each other, over remedies and rhubarb, over taking cold, over draughts and diets, just as they do everywhere. *Emma* is full of the very ordinariness of such conversations and events, but whilst giving us this rich ordinariness, the novel at the same time infuses them with extraordinary narrative tension and excitement. Gossip and talk about health, highlighted extensively in the great comic dialogue in Chapter 12 in which Isabella and her father dispute the rival virtues of their favourite doctors and health resorts, is more than a source of incidental humour in the novel, one might suggest. It has a larger and more important dimension.

This is because the notion of health asks to be understood in a moral register as well as in a physical one, though the two are interconnected. The focus of this is Emma herself. The reader is introduced to Emma Woodhouse through being privy to her own consciousness, sharing her excitement at the pleasure, the game, that taking up Harriet Smith promises (23). At the same time, through the irony that the technique of free indirect discourse allows, the reader necessarily feels quite severe doubts about Emma's reasoning and motives. This mixed response to Emma's enthusiasm for Harriet is soon taken up and spelt out in the conversation between Mr Knightley and Mrs Weston in Chapter 5. One speaks of his reservations about her, the other replies by pointing out how lovely Emma is—that she is 'the complete picture of grown-up health' (39). Mrs Weston's response is superficially illogical, and doesn't meet Mr Knightley's criticisms, but at a deeper level, it does, because by speaking of Emma as 'the picture of health' Mrs Weston indicates her sense of Emma's fundamental or ontological goodness—that she is not only physically, but also emotionally and morally sound.

It's this principle of health in Emma Woodhouse that is the source of the novel's energy and warmth. For most of the book, 'spirited', capable and active, as she is, she has no difficulty in coping with the dogged timidity and resistances of her father. His ill-health (real or presumed) is also understood in a moral as well as a physical sense. He is frightened of draughts, of even short journeys in the carriage, of anything unpredictable or unforeseen or hasty. 'To have any of them sitting down out of doors to eat would inevitably make him ill', as Mr Knightley surmises (356). It would be too melodramatic, and out of harmony with the spirit of the novel, to say that he is afraid of life itself, but to put it that way suggests how the stakes in *Emma* are quite high. His invalidism is not difficult to think of as an emotional and characterological constriction or failure—and if 'eager' is one of the novel's most frequent characterising words for its heroine, by confronting that eagerness with its opposite, with invalidism and withdrawal, a profound and central ethical conflict is set up.

Another figure clearly contrasted with Emma in this respect is Jane Fairfax. 'Bless me! poor Jane is ill!' is Miss Bates's first exclamation when reading the letter that introduces her into the novel (166). This association of Jane with ill-health always shadows her, although in this instance one might share Emma's suspicion that Jane's cold is no more than a convenient pretext for her return to Highbury. But the theme of Jane's liability to illness is continued when Mr Knightley steps in to prevent her from singing herself hoarse (229) or when his brother John takes it upon himself to comment on her walking in the rain. These chivalrous interventions however are not all that they seem, for it is as if the motif of Jane's ill-health gathers together a whole set of anxieties concerned with specifically female vulnerability. Whilst Jane is thus figured as the opposite to that Emma who responds to Mrs Weston's query 'Are you well, my Emma?' with 'Oh! perfectly, I am always well, you know' (420), she is also capable of representing something about the limits and conditions of a lady's life. Jane's ill-health or the threat of it, is also a way of defining the cloud that hangs over her, the confinement of her condition, the stresses and constrictions involved in dwelling with her aunt. Miss Fairfax is pale, subject to prolonged nervous tension and anxiety, and at the climax of the novel undergoes a collapse which is clearly more emotional than physical, as Mr Perry, at this late stage of the book revealing himself as a wise and trustworthy clinician, perceives. His speech is still reported, not direct: 'Her present home, he could not but observe, was unfavourable to a nervous disorder: confined always to one room;—he could have wished it otherwise' (389). The victim of repression and anxiety, Jane is cured, as Mrs Elton archly remarks, by 'a young physician from Richmond', Frank Churchill.

In the structure of the novel Frank is homologous with Emma. His difficulties with the erratic and demanding hypochondriac Mrs Churchill are a distant reflection of hers with Mr Woodhouse. Mrs Churchill's influence acts to restrict and frustrate his erotic life in a way that parallels Mr Woodhouse's effect on Emma, though in a more material and sharper way. Like Emma, Frank is never ill. He is a figure of energy in the text, of a restless (and inevitably sexual) spiritedness that is the more frenetic, erratic, the more reckless, the more it is frustrated. His teasing, ingenuity and contrivance matches Emma's and signals to the reader that her own stratagems may well have a physical underpinning. Initially his energy is diverted into his ingenious schemes to snatch opportunities to be with Jane, partly in his amusement at hoodwinking the delightful, but to him not sexually alluring, Miss Woodhouse. His energy is expressed not only in his physical activity (he rides about the countryside a lot) but also his schemes and plans, like the ball at the Crown Inn. It's very characteristic that when, finally blocked by Jane's apparent resolution in breaking off their engagement at Box Hill, he thinks of more movement, in a wider sphere, of going abroad. His frustration communicates itself to Emma. 'The young man's spirits now rose to a pitch almost unpleasant' (374).

Frank Churchill and Mr Woodhouse meet head on over the plans for the ball at the Crown. Where the preparations for the dance are concerned Mr Woodhouse is as vocal and determined as he is anywhere in the novel. He is afraid of them all catching colds from the damp rooms inevitably found at an inn, and says so. Frank cannot resist:

> 'I was going to observe, Sir', said Frank Churchill, 'that one of
> the great recommendations of this change would be the very little

danger of any body's catching cold—so much less danger at the Crown than at Randalls! Mr Perry might regret the alteration, but nobody else could.'

'Sir', said Mr Woodhouse, rather warmly, 'you are very much mistaken if you suppose Mr Perry to be that sort of character. Mr Perry is extremely concerned when any of us is ill. But I do not understand how the room at the Crown can be safer for you than your father's house.'

'From the very circumstance of its being larger, sir. We shall have no occasion to open the windows at all—not once the whole evening; and it is that dreadful habit of opening the windows, letting in cold air upon heated bodies, which (as you well know, sir) does the mischief.'

'Open the windows! But surely, Mr Churchill, nobody would think of opening the windows at Randalls. Nobody could be so imprudent! I never heard of such a thing. Dancing with open windows!—I am sure, neither your father nor Mrs Weston (poor Miss Taylor that was) would suffer it.'

'Ah Sir, but a thoughtless young person will sometimes step behind a window-curtain and throw up a sash, without its being suspected. I have often known it done myself.'

'Have you indeed sir—Bless me! I never could have supposed it. But I live out of the world and am often astonished at what I hear.' (251–2)

It is comic scenes like this that give *Emma* its distinctive quality. Ostensibly this dialogue is about physical health, but it is not hard to show that it is about much more than that. Frank's teasing is similar to, but more amiable (if more persistent) than Mr John Knightley's earlier taunting about the dangers of snow on the ground at Randalls. It's at this point that what Frank here stands for—youth, energy, enterprise—is most directly confronted with Mr Woodhouse's conservatism, once again enlisting Mr Perry, the hidden centre of the novel's circling concern with health.

Moreover at this point a key association link between health, creativity and the materially real 'open' or closed environment is suggested. Oliver Sacks has remarked that the defining condition of patienthood is 'the contraction in all realms (not least the moral realm)' and pointed conversely to 'the spaciousness of health, of full being, of the real world'.[1] This association of illness with contracture, of health with spaciousness, is translated in *Emma* into actual settings and environments. *Emma* is a novel which begins with scenes of confinement within doors that gradually diminish in frequency, as the seasons turn from winter to spring to summer, and the action bells out, the pace heats up, with occasions and expeditions. The symbolic freight or associations of indoor and outdoor settings is hinted too in such characterising declarations in the novel as 'I love an open nature', and 'Oh, if you knew how much I love everything that is decided and open!' (460). Naturally some readers, or a part of every reader, will feel that this talk about opening windows is a rather cruel and irresponsible teasing of the old gentleman, but most, I think, will recognise that our laughter is on Frank's part—that, for all his delight in mischief, he is speaking for health.

Health in *Emma* then has a spatial or material register too. In many ways, the novel suggests, health may be a more problematic matter for women than for men, for ladies than for gentlemen. Men ride about freely, to London and back in a day, or walk three miles round to pick walnuts. A lady cannot walk across the street to get letters in a light rain without attracting the kindly but interfering attention of her neighbours. The drawing room and the garden is her province. It could be said of course that Jane Austen is here merely reflecting the manners and customs of her time, but there is more to it than that. The novel connects health and energy with activity and the outdoors; indoors is associated with the stifling of energies and enterprise. The novel wants us to make a connection between confinement and ill-health (of the psychosomatic kind), and to suggest how health has some necessary connection with outgoing or openness, in all of its senses. The moments of freedom, when a woman is alone and able to walk at leisure outside, are treasured spaces in the novel: they define some of its highest points. 'Oh, Miss Woodhouse, the comfort of being sometimes alone!' Jane Fairfax exclaims when being pushed to extreme and unladylike measures she flees the strawberry party at Donwell. Here 'comfort', associated for so much of the novel with the indoors, becomes transformed into a value that overrides those conditions, paradoxically existing through solitude, freedom, exercise of free will and physical activity. 'Quick walking will refresh me,' pleads Jane (363).

This is not by any means the novel's only use of the word. Running alongside the novel's focus on health, in fact, is its attention to 'comfort'.[2] Emma's 'comfortable home' is mentioned in the very first sentence, and the word, or its cognates, recurs continually, making its unobtrusive contribution to the novel's special ambience and network of ideas. No doubt it stands for something that Jane Austen herself valued dearly. In a letter soon after she and her mother and sister had arrived at Chawton cottage in 1809, she used it in quick association with the idea of having a settled domicile at last. 'Cassandra's pen,' she writes, 'will paint our state, / The many comforts that await / Our Chawton home. . . .'[3] All three of the novels written, or completed, at Chawton testify to the importance Austen attached to the notion of home, and to the provision of domestic comfort.[4] The word had acquired its dominant modern senses by the time Austen wrote. In earlier centuries the noun 'comfort' meant 'assistance or support' and its associated verb took the same colouring: 'Be comfortable to my mother, your mistress, and make much of her,' are Bertram's parting words to Helena in Shakespeare's *All's Well That Ends Well* (c. 1602). In Johnson's *Dictionary* of 1755, comfort is still defined as meaning 'consolation, support under calamity or danger'. 'Comfort' evolved its domestic meaning in the later eighteenth century in tandem with the development of a more leisured society: it is an indisputably middle-class or bourgeois notion, depending as it usually does upon a material substrate, a steady income, for the security, placidity and ease it evolved to denote.

When we look at the dozens of references to comfort in *Emma* we find that the word is sometimes used with this material meaning uppermost, as when Mrs Weston's 'comfortable provision' is mentioned or when Mr Weston is said to have 'fitted up his house so comfortably' (13). But when Emma guiltily reflects that she has failed to add to 'the stock of the Bates's scanty comforts' (155), by not visiting them as often as she should, it is clear that the novelist employs the word to cover a far broader range of meaning. If Emma thinks sardonically about Harriet's admiration for 'the many comforts and wonders of Abbey Mill farm', she is using the word in one of its oldest senses, meaning, according to the O.E.D., 'enjoyment and delight'. Frank Churchill, in front of the Eltons' house, comments that if it were to be shared with the woman he loved, the vicarage, though small, must have ample room 'for every real comfort' (204). We hear too of Mr Woodhouse's 'comfortable talk with his dear Isabella'. Mr Perry seems to dispense comfort in this sense as well as medicines in his consultations with Mr Woodhouse (434).

'Comfort' then is clearly a concept with a wide range of suggestive-ness. Whilst it points to a key value not only of the community depicted in the novel, but of the novel itself, it also rings alarm bells. Young readers will not need alerting to the idea that a world devoted to comfort, above all, is a world that has turned its back on risk, adventure, excitement. It is a seduc-tive and problematic value. It allows no conceptual space for movement, for enterprise, for the strong, the heroic, the romantic. If one were to say that *Emma* celebrates the values of comfort one would be acquiescing in a view of Jane Austen not unlike that notoriously expressed by Charlotte Brontë.[5] Yet it is plain that the word does spring to Austen's pen when she seeks to define something important and to be treasured. In one of the novel's more remarkable references Emma thinks of it in salutation of the landscape before her at Donwell Abbey, 'It was a sweet view—sweet to the eye and to the mind. English verdure, English culture, English comfort, seen under a sun bright, without being oppressive' (360). It is striking, once again, that Austen uses a word so much coloured by associations with the indoors to define her heroine's deepest moment of affiliation with a beloved landscape, as part of temperately phrased but none the less absolute endorsement of her commu-nion with the qualities that landscape bodies forth. (This is three pages before Jane Fairfax is to invoke 'the comfort of being alone!') Even so, comfort is a value that might make a modern reader, so to speak, uncomfortable. It is cer-tainly in some ways rather difficult to reconcile with that enhanced sense of health which, as I've been arguing, the novel makes pivotal to its argument.

One primary focus of comfort in *Emma* in fact is on Mr Woodhouse. 'Her father's comfort' is one of the constant preoccupations of even the Emma who with another part of her mind is busily playing imaginative games with Harriet Smith and Mr Elton and later with Jane Fairfax and Mr Dixon. 'To her he looked for comfort' (127). 'Comfort' in Mr Woodhouse's sense means only habit, familiarity, safety, a reassurance that is premised upon compensa-tion for an unspoken or unacknowledged loss. It is a substitutive value, a consolation or solace, a secondary replacement for a failure, an emptiness, that cannot be defined. The question marks around comfort are prominent in John Knightley's unwillingness ever to leave home ('the folly of not allowing people to be comfortable at home') or when Mrs Elton pronounces platitudi-nously 'There is nothing like staying at home for real comfort' (274).

The problematic side of this value though emerges most sharply when Emma tells Harriet early in the novel that she will never marry since her nephews and nieces will 'supply every sort of sensation that declining life can need' and that such attachments 'suit' her 'ideas of comfort better than what is warmer and blinder' (86). At this point, it becomes especially clear that the cultivation of comfort (however broad a meaning the word may be made to carry) can be, in no very esoteric sense, self-destroying, shutting down options and denying aspects of the personality that are demonstrated in the charac-ter's vigour and decisiveness even as she speaks. Comfort also suggests a kind of dependency, something that is in strong contrast to that native energy or creative spark that is signalled so strongly when Emma is described and nar-ratively incarnated as 'the picture of health'.

But this is far from all the novel has to say about comfort. One of the most interesting moments in which comfort is at issue in *Emma* occurs after Harriet Smith has suddenly come upon the Martins in Mrs Ford's shop. Her emotions are as confused as her grammar: 'Oh! Miss Woodhouse, I would rather done any thing than have it happen: and yet, you know, there was a sort of satisfac-tion in seeing him behave so pleasantly and so kindly. And Elizabeth, too, Oh! Miss Woodhouse, do talk to me and make me comfortable again.' Harriet is obviously in one sense asking to be treated as a child, 'comforted' in the sense of soothed and cossetted. But the appeal goes deeper than this, as one can see by the confusion of Emma's response. 'Very sincerely did Emma wish to do so; but it was not immediately in her power. She was obliged to stop and think. She was not thoroughly comfortable herself' (179). Emma cannot meet Harriet's demands fully, cannot respond with the unqualified acceptance of a mother, because she is herself disturbed. The encounter, as Harriet recounts it, stirs up her conscience. So though she 'exerts herself, and did try to make her comfortable, by considering all that had passed as a mere trifle, and quite unworthy of being dwelt on', this tactic is doomed to failure. Brushing both her own and Harriet's disturbance under the carpet, Emma does not address the deeper sources of Harriet's unhappiness, and so she is condemned to hear Harriet harp on the same theme for a while yet. She cannot give comfort in the deeper, more august sense that the passage also invokes. In the psychoanalyst D.W. Winnicott's phrase, she is 'not there to receive the communication': not 'there' because she is distracted by her own needs. She cannot 'hold' or 'contain' Harriet's distress and therefore cannot communicate calmness or acceptance to her friend. She cannot give a soothing that is also sustenance.

In contrast is the occasion some time later when Harriet is in a rather similar 'flutter of spirits' over Mr Elton's wedding (Volume II, Chapter 13). In this case, Emma is very clear about what she thinks, and admits her own part in Harriet's unhappiness—'Deceived myself, I did very miserably deceive you' she says with characteristic directness (268). She appeals to Harriet's love for her, and to her own pride; 'the violence of grief was comforted away', and the cure is lasting. Emma here performs the function of the good parent or mother: accepting her friend's 'unhappiness', and her own guilt, she is able to offer a kind of sustenance that arises out of her own candour and self-knowledge, a psychological 'support', that is born out of her own inner resilience and health. As these interchanges make clear, the notion of comfort moves beyond the material, and beyond compensatory and suspect 'comfort' of the sick. 'Comfort' at this point no longer has an uneasy relation to health, but seems to be a consequence of it. So we should not despise Jane Austen's attention to comfort and the comfortable in this novel.

The novel's interest in health and illness, in activity and stasis, in the indoors and the outdoors, all of which are linked and melded together, is demonstrated most moving in the staging of Emma and Mr Knightley's final reconciliation in Volume III, Chapter 13 (or 49 in modern editions). When it looks as though Harriet and Mr Knightley might marry Emma experiences her most melancholy evening, pacing about the drawing room at Hartfield, full of ominous thoughts, an evening during which her father 'could only be kept tolerably comfortable by . . . exertions which had never cost her half so much before' (422). Emma's energies are here in danger of being overtaxed, consumed by the domestic affections that whilst they are certainly part of those qualities in her that may be trusted (as Mrs Weston has put it) are in another sense the very avenues through which her young life's own project may be stemmed and frustrated. But the next day the weather clears.

> With all the eagerness which such a transition gives, Emma resolved to be out of doors as soon as possible. Never had the exquisite sight, smell, sensation of nature, tranquil, warm and brilliant after a storm, been more attractive to her. She longed for the serenity they might gradually introduce; and on Mr Perry's coming in soon after dinner, with a disengaged hour to give to her father, she lost no time in hurrying into the shrubbery. (424)

The claims of comfort and health are exquisitely balanced in this climactic scene. With her father indoors, taken care of, comfortably occupied with Mr Perry, Emma is free to step outdoors, to be creative—to take those courageous and playful conversational initiatives that culminate in the clearing up of mutual misunderstandings, and lead Mr Knightley towards his declaration of love. Emma's health is thus understood, as Winnicott understood it, against a background of containing stability. Her creativity flourishes, as did Austen's as an artist, not despite, but because her 'world'—in Austen's case, cultural tradition, and family loyalty—is there in place reliably to hold and assist her. Winnicott made no bones about the significance of conception of psychological health he propounds, calling it 'the essential central element of creative originality'. There are many, many, different ways in which the greatness, the humour, the intricacy, the romance, the vigour of *Emma* can be brought out, and what I have suggested here is merely one way of configuring the novel. But there is no way round the fact that if *Emma* is an enduring masterpiece that is because it addresses issues that are at the centre of life, and of health, itself.

NOTES

1. Oliver Sacks, *A Leg to Stand On*, London: Picador, 1985, p. 125.
2. See Chapter 5, 'Ease' in Witold Rybczynski, *Home: A short history of an idea*, New York: Viking Penguin, 1986, pp. 101–121, especially, pp. 120–121.
3. Letter to Francis Austen, 26 July 1809.
4. Joy Alexander counts at least 129 occurrences of comfort or its derivatives in *Mansfield Park*. She shows how in that novel the word ranges in meaning from 'being cossetted' to the older sense of 'being strengthened and consoled', with Fanny Price filling the role of the Comforter; Joy Alexander, 'Anything Goes? Reading *Mansfield Park*', *The Use of English*, 52, 3, 2001, pp. 239–51.
5. 'No fresh air, no blue hill, no bonny beck. I should hardly like to live with her ladies and gentlemen, in their elegant but confined houses', Letter to G.H. Lewes, 12 January 1848; 'she ruffles her reader by nothing vehement, disturbs him by nothing profound'. Letter to W.S. Williams, 12 April 1850: etc.

IVOR MORRIS

The Enigma of Harriet Smith

Our puzzlement over Harriet Smith begins at the first mention of her. She is introduced as "the natural daughter of somebody," who years before had placed her at Mrs. Goddard's school, where her situation is now that of parlour-boarder. And the action of one of the world's great novels is to turn round the girl pursuing this humble existence: upon her capacity to engage the affections successively of an Elton, a Churchill, a Knightley. The story's credibility and effectiveness, no less, depends on its sustaining the reader's impression that she has qualities which can or will overcome her social deficiency. It takes the shock of Harriet's potential power over Mr. Knightley to awaken Emma to her love for him—and the reality of the distress thus aroused to halt in memorable fashion his proposing to her, in terror lest he should be at the point of confessing an attachment to her protégée. Throughout the novel runs an insistent questioning, whether explicit or unspoken: is Harriet a commendable young woman, a lady in the making—or is she not?

Once she has met Harriet, Emma appears to be certain. She wastes no time, we are told, "in inviting, encouraging and telling her to come very often" to Hartfield (26), resolved to give her the needed sophistication. She has not found her to be clever; but while strength of understanding could not be imparted, Harriet's evident appreciation of what was elegant and witty,

From *Persuasions* 26, no. 1 (Winter 2005). © 2005 by the Jane Austen Society of North America.

her ready embracing of a style of living previously unknown to her, showed that she must have good sense and deserve encouragement. In Emma's first estimation, this was a girl "who only wanted a little more knowledge and elegance to be quite perfect" (23).

The term raises more doubt than it settles. Other than providing herself with an acceptable walking companion, is it Emma's intention to create an agreeable but lesser being, or one who will by these attentions graduate to true estimableness?

An answer is surely present in the fact of what Emma is doing. It is on the face of it unlikely that a woman of her accomplishment would select someone unworthy of her friendship and favour. For Emma is if anything distinguished amongst Jane Austen's heroines by a discernment as to persons in terms both general and particular. Take, for instance, her comment upon Churchill's sudden journeying to London for a haircut, that "'silly things do cease to be silly if they are done by sensible people in an impudent way'": it is a real insight into human conduct (212). And when, earlier, she has countered Churchill's assertion that no one can be attracted by a reserved character with the retort, "'Not till the reserve ceases towards oneself; and then the attraction may be the greater,'" she is as near as may be to divining the secret of his engagement to Jane Fairfax, which his remark was intended to conceal (203).

Amidst the flow of happenings in Highbury, Emma displays a quick apprehension of motive. She recognises the presence of "great fear, great caution, great resolution" in Jane's determining to stay at her aunt's (285); senses a new happiness after her collecting letters from the post office; and detects her embarrassment at the gift of the piano, and "very reprehensible feelings" as she begins to press the keys (243). The notion that Knightley might be the piano's donor, or that he might care romantically about Jane, is as incisively dismissed as is his own professed indifference to whether he arrives at a dinner party on foot, or by coach as properly he should (226, 213). And, despite the force of her initial attraction to Churchill, Emma is soon sure that there can be no building upon "steadiness or constancy" in his disposition, and of her own undoubted preference not amounting to affection for him (265). His engaging manner towards her upon his reappearance in Highbury, further, does not conceal from her a restlessness, "a liveliness that did not satisfy himself," which betokens a lessening of interest in herself—though she is mistaken, and understandably so, in putting it down to a fear of the effect of her personal charms (316).

The same percipient regard plays constantly upon Harriet. It is with an amused, ironic detachment that Emma contemplates "the many vacancies" of her mind (183), and what Sir Thomas Bertram would have described as her "rusticities" of demeanour. Harriet's being nearly recovered from her cold inspires in Emma a wish "that she should have as much time as possible for getting the better of her other complaint," or else "mania," such being her estimate of her young friend's feelings for Mr. Elton. But the emotion as such Emma is far from scorning: she is herself much affected by the artlessness of Harriet's grief when she has disclosed to her the truth of Elton's indifference, and the extent of her own error. But it is not without significance that, in the depth of her conviction at this point, "Harriet was the superior creature of the two—and that to resemble her would be more for her own happiness than all that genius and intelligence could do," Emma can keep her sympathies in check with the wry thought that it was rather too late in the day "to set about being simple-minded and ignorant" (141–42). The surmise might be held as indication enough that her decision over Harriet will not have been other than clear-sighted.

* * *

However, there is evidence of a very different order regarding Emma: that while discernment in her is plentiful, her judgment is liable on occasion to impulsive aberration. She shows herself capable of both wilfully suppressing better knowledge, and reversing her opinion without the least awareness of having done so. The matter of the haircut provides an excellent example of the first. Troubled by its air of "foppery and nonsense," she finds Churchill guilty of vanity, extravagance, and the like, but also more seriously open to the charge of ungentlemanliness in his disregard of the Westons' feelings, and unconcern as to the impression his behaviour might more generally give rise to. Upon hearing, though, of his highly favourable reception in High-bury, as well as at Randalls, and, from Mr. Weston, how "very beautiful and very charming" he considers her to be, Emma finds that "she must not judge him harshly" (205–06). Nor, when the idea of a ball at Randalls is under discussion, is she able to condemn the lack of gallantry in his studiously ignoring her protest against "'a crowd in a little room!'" while professing admiration of the phrase. Attributing his persistence to a wish not to lose the pleasure of dancing with her, "she took the compliment, and forgave the rest" (249–50).

Emma's dealings with both the Martins and the Coles are tergiversation itself. The former family, she tells herself at the start, must be coarse and unpolished, quite unworthy of their previous association with her little friend; and as for Mr. Martin when she casts eyes upon him, he "looked as if he did not know what manner was," being, as she proceeds to inform the mortified Harriet, "'so very clownish, so totally without air.'" Her considering, at the end, that "It would be a great pleasure to know Robert Martin," reveals her attitude to have been founded on pure prejudice (475). With the Coles it is much the same, except that they do not have to wait so long for the change to come about. Their invitation to the gentry Emma at first strongly reprehends. Such persons "ought to be taught that it was not for them to arrange the terms on which the superior families would visit them"—though the lesson, she very much fears, will come only from herself. Strangely, however, the prospect of aloofness affords her no contentment, the yielding of her peers demolishes her resistance: and recollection of the dinner party next day is graced with the persuasion that by her presence she must have delighted the Coles—"worthy people—who deserved to be made happy!—And left a name behind her that would not soon die away" (207, 231).

These inconsistencies, while perhaps laudable in denoting the softening of positions that were unduly severe, could scarcely be more evident. They are, it should be noted, in part the outcome of an inability in Emma to tolerate "'a subjection of the fancy to the understanding,'" as Knightley has it (37). In the author's terms, she is "an imaginist": one whose lively mind and unacknowledged feelings can construct "a ground-work of anticipation" for what might prove either fact or fantasy, and cause the last to be treated as substantive (335).

More than this, engaged as she is in influencing Harriet beneath an appearance of neutrality, Emma is herself subject to a powerful impulsion she can have no idea of, since it arises out of her own disposition. It reveals itself in her besetting imperative of how best to exercise her social superiority. Eminence might be the better word, for Highbury "afforded her no equals," the Woodhouses being first in consequence there. And it is not status alone which makes for self-approval: Emma enjoys full awareness of her claims of personality and intellect. She can boast of having from the start planned the match between Miss Taylor and Mr. Weston, and rejoice at the thought of how "'such success has blessed me'" (12); and in calmer vein can as hostess demonstrate the "real good-will of a mind delighted with its own ideas" (24), and as a daughter contemplate the benefits of such an affection in her father "as could never find fault" (6).

Might it be that these promptings in *Emma* combine to evoke instant approval for the girl who upon introduction displays "so proper and becoming a deference" to her, and appears "so pleasantly grateful" for her condescension, and "artlessly impressed" with Hartfield's—and its mistress's—grandeur: whose appreciative response is little less than tribute to all that Emma is, or takes herself to be? For from that moment she is afire with the purpose that is to direct her course through the novel, upon which her every instinct appears to be employed.

She would notice her; she would improve her; she would detach her from her bad acquaintance, and introduce her into good society; she would form her opinions and manners. It would be an interesting, and certainly a very kind undertaking; highly becoming her own situation in life, her leisure, and powers. (23–24)

The aim of Harriet's improvement is to be achieved by the simple means of association with her patroness: mere acceptance is seen as conferring an immediate dignity and worth. It is not therefore surprising that Emma's first remark on hearing of Mr. Martin's proposing to Harriet should be upon his evident determination to "'connect himself well if he can'" (50); or that she should respond to Knightley's vexation later at the young man's being refused with the deprecatory coolness of "'I cannot admit him to be Harriet's equal.'" And Knightley's counter-claim thereupon of its being a beneficial offer for Harriet is met with the incensed reply, "'a good match for my intimate friend!'" (61–62). This is the outcry of someone as entrenched in the concept of her own superiority as Lady Catherine de Bourgh; and it supports the possibility that Emma's appraisal of Harriet has been unconsciously affected by the idea of her own status and capabilities: that she has viewed her protégée through the distorting glass of her estimate of herself.

In one respect, at least, the above cannot apply: Harriet's remarkable prettiness is beyond dispute. It may be "of a sort which Emma particularly admired" (23), but corroboration is forthcoming from many other observers. There is a certain wonder in Knightley's comment to Mrs. Weston that Emma appears very little concerned with her own handsomeness. She in fact seems more preoccupied with the looks of other women: Jane Austen has endowed her with a distinctive regard for feminine beauty. During her welcoming visit to Jane Fairfax, Emma sits looking at her with the "complacency" which Jane's "very pleasing beauty" inspires. Elegance is its predominant feature; and when afterwards Churchill makes so bold as to belittle it, she is astonished to the point of concluding with some scorn that there must be a very distinct sort of elegance in the fashionable world he belongs to if Jane Fairfax is to be thought "only ordinarily gifted with it" (167, 194).

Emma indeed appears most in accord with Churchill, and as it were mentally attuned to him, when he is itemising Jane's charms to her during their reconciliation at the Westons'. The sentiment of Alexander Pope, that "Fair tresses man's imperial race ensnare, / And beauty draws us with a single hair," would have gained her enthusiastic approval. Can it be, therefore, that Harriet's fine bloom, blue eyes, light hair, regular features and look of "great sweetness" are in effect an assault upon Emma's objectivity, and that "those soft blue eyes" (23–24) are all the while leading her into idealizing their possessor for graces not present in her: that, through an excessive preoccupation with what is outward in Harriet, to say nothing of other sources of misapprehension, Emma has come to be quite deluded in her regard for her protégée?

* * *

Emma's lifelong acquaintance and future husband certainly thinks so. His view of Harriet, imparted even in the civil tones of his address to Mrs. Weston, is unequivocal. Her companionship will be positively harmful to Emma through the "'hourly flattery'" that a nature so ignorant will render. She herself will gain only a little polish from the proximity; the "'strength of mind'" which she sorely needs Emma will be unable to bestow (38–39). This assertion is but a prelude, however, to the scathing assessment Knightley delivers upon discovery of Emma's part in Harriet's declining Martin's proposal. She is a girl of little sense and no information, who is totally lacking in experience, "'and, with her little wit, is not very likely ever to have any that can avail her.'" A prospective lover would face the impediments of "'illegitimacy and ignorance'"; and Harriet's continued association with Emma will only bring about in her the mischief which "'Vanity working on a weak head produces'" (61–64).

But this somewhat less than favourable judgment undergoes distinct moderation with the passage of time. Upon Emma's being constrained to confess to him how much Mr. Elton has fallen in her estimation, the gratified Knightley is moved to declare that her friend has greatly risen in his, especially through comparison with the woman Elton has lately taken to wife. He has discerned Harriet to possess "'some first rate qualities'" which the former Augusta Hawkins is without, amongst them a modest, unassuming nature which makes her "'infinitely to be preferred'" by any man of sense—who would moreover find, as he has done, that she is "'more conversable'" than at first appears (331).

True, this is not yet praise of the glowing sort; and some further qualification might be assumed in Knightley's suggestion, in accounting for Harriet's prompt acceptance of Martin upon their meeting in Brunswick Square, that a good-tempered, soft-hearted girl such as she was "'not likely to be very, very determined against any young man who told her he loved her'" (473). But persuadableness in a young woman, even in a matter of such seriousness, was in that age deemed a virtue, a fact strongly impressed upon the reluctant Catherine Morland and Fanny Price: and had not Knightley himself jestingly taunted Mrs. Weston with it, in respect of the schooling which the young Emma had subjected her to? And on this occasion he is overlooking Harriet's early preference. What though is apparent is that, by the end, his initial disapproval of her has vanished.

No such reversal occurs in Emma's thinking. What she asserts about Harriet during the painful interview which followed Martin's being refused is sustained through all that follows; indeed, there is even to be seen in her a heightening of regard for her young charge. Not that she ever comes to imagine Harriet intelligent: but she remains assured that the girl has "'better sense'" than Knightley is aware of. The same is true of the prettiness and good nature which he has discounted. These attributes Emma cannot believe to be trivial: the former, she tells him, will hold sway over men until such time as "'they do fall in love with well-informed minds instead of handsome faces'"; and the latter cannot fail of being a universal recommendation. In her uniting the two, she affirms, Harriet is "'exactly what every man delights in'": and were he ever to marry, "'she is the very woman for you'" (63–64).

The last utterance is a riposte, made with jocularity and abandon by an Emma under attack from her formidable opponent. But that it springs from conviction is proved by the manner, later on, in which Harriet's confiding her hopes of Knightley is received. The overpowering sensation in Emma is of course what springs from sudden discovery of her own love; but, this set aside—if it may be—her dominant concern at the news is the consequence for himself if he were to marry beneath him: as she pictures it afterwards, "the smiles, the sneers, the merriment it would prompt at his expense" (413). Neither in Harriet herself, nor in the evidence of his fondness she puts forward, does Emma find grounds for dismissing Knightley's attachment as improbable through personal deficiency in its object. The disparity in qualities, as in rank, she is painfully aware of; yet, "Was it a new circumstance for a man of first-rate abilities to be captivated by very inferior powers?" It is very clear that in her own thoughts Emma accords Harriet the full status of a rival: that she sees her in all her attractiveness as little less than the incarnation of her own outlook and philosophy upon womankind.

To this conclusion, however, it might be objected that Emma's mind at the time is not capable of any objective assessment. She is in the grip of new and tyrannical emotions: the desire to possess, accompanied by the terror of losing. Love and fear exert their full force; and, were this not enough, she is all the while being afflicted by the bewildering recognition of "[t]he blunders, the blindness of her own head and heart!" (411–12). The state is one which, in her apprehension, would invest the plainest of plain Janes with the enchantments of a siren.

When, much later on, assured of the man she loves, and responding to life in the glow of the heart's fulfillment, she expresses to Knightley a wish for the happiness of the betrothed Harriet and Martin, Emma answers his cryptic observation upon the change she has undergone since they last talked on the subject with the self-accusation, "'at that time I was a fool.'" It would be unwise to take the emphatic remark as a confession of disenchantment with Harriet. It is acknowledgement, rather, of Knightley's having been correct in his view of the sphere that life and fortune had marked out for the girl, and of her own lapse in having so romantically departed from the prevailing conventions she is now re-converted to. Here also, therefore, she is not in suitable mood to pronounce upon Harriet's promise. No more, evidently, is Knightley himself, in the indeterminate approval he then voices as to her being "'an artless, amiable girl, with very good notions, very seriously good principles, and placing her happiness in the affections and utility of domestic life'" (474). If there is apology of a sort in these words, repentance has been present in Emma's little outburst, for the presumption she was guilty of in taking it upon herself to direct another's destiny, and the blunders and embarrassments it has involved them in. The matter of Harriet's personableness—her fitness to attach a man of some consequence, and gain respectability in the world Jane Austen's novels reflect—is left still to be determined.

* * *

The question arises whether Harriet's moderate mental powers would be a hindrance. Emma sees the want of cleverness as adverse; and our own early impressions are of a thoughtlessness and indecision implicit in the "'Oh, dear, no'" and "'Oh! dear, yes!'" of Harriet's hasty assents during their first walk (87), the see-saw response to Emma's inference that Mr. Martin does not read—"'Oh, yes!—that is, no—I do not know—but I believe he has read a good deal—but not what you would think anything of'" (29)—and the agonising at Ford's as to the destination of the purchased muslin and ribbon.

These are minor issues—but not so the cause which brings Harriet with all speed to ask advice upon her receipt of Martin's letter. Emma, we are told, is even half ashamed of her young friend "for seeming so pleased and so doubtful" upon such a theme. The doubt persists throughout their interview, Emma's approval of the letter on perusing it, and inquiry as to whether the answer is to be favourable, gaining little more than a "'well—and—and what shall I do?'" and a "'What would you advise me to do? Pray, dear Miss Woodhouse, tell me what I ought to do?'" And when, after being with solemn propriety cautioned that marriage is not a proper state to be entered into "'with half a heart,'" and questioned as to Mr. Martin's being "'the most agreeable man'" she has ever been in company with, Harriet is propelled to a decision, it is couched in terms which reveal it as a lesser triumph of equivocation: "'and I have now quite determined, and really almost made up my mind—to refuse Mr. Martin. Do you think I am right?'" (50–53).

But indecision at a first proposal is entirely fitting in Harriet's case. She is scarcely out of school, "a green girl / Unsifted in such perilous circumstance"; and one, further, whose origins have precluded the ambience and support of a family, as they have acquaintance with the modes of decorum in the imposing world to which she has been so extraordinarily elevated. What is more natural than that Martin's declaration should enhance the sense of her solitariness, and cause her fearfully to seek counsel and comfort from the greatness that has befriended her?

In whatever context she is finally settled, Harriet will not be renowned for resource and positiveness in reasoning. Her capacities as displayed in the novel are limited, from the instance of her wondering whether the solution of Elton's charade is a "'trident? or a mermaid? or a shark?'" (73) to its being "'very odd'" that there should be a fortnight and a day's difference between Mr. Martin's birthday and her own (30), or her finding it almost conclusive that Martin's letter of proposal is mere prose, in comparison to the verse of the charade (76). In the latter instances, though, we are encountering the force of affection—as we are in Harriet's tempering the admission of Jane Fairfax's playing being perhaps superior to Emma's with the consoling irrelevance that "'if she does play so very well, you know, it is no more than she is obliged to do, because she will have to teach'"; or in her designating, and actually enshrining, Elton's bit of plaster and pencil-end as "*Most precious treasures.*" Her distaste for Italian singing upon the plea that "'There is no understanding a word of it'" can, however, admit no such extenuation (232). And if her logic is more admissible when she reacts to Emma's declared resolution never to marry, it springs from the commonplace notions of its being unusual to hear a young woman say such a thing, and "'so dreadful'" to end up an old maid.

Be this as it may, amidst society at any level Harriet appears a lively and personable presence, taking a keen interest in all its manifestations. Possessions as such excite her, whether the Martins' "'very handsome summer house, large enough to hold a dozen people,'" or their "'two parlours, two very good parlours indeed'"—or even the "'beautiful goose'" Mrs. Martin presents to Mrs. Goddard. But it is people who truly hold her interest. She can, for example, speak with the same "exultation" of Mrs. Martin's having "'an upper maid who had lived five-and-twenty years with her'" (27–28); and she is most freely herself when concerned with the sayings and doings of others. In the recital of her being discovered by Miss Nash peeping with the two Abbots through the blind at Mr. Elton, and their being scolded away from the window only for Miss Nash to take their place and then good-naturedly call her back to let her see too, and their confiding to each other "'how beautiful we thought he looked!'" Harriet is at her liveliest (75).

She is so again when repeating to Emma, "with great delight," what Miss Nash had told her about Mr. Perry's meeting with Mr. Elton on the road to London, and being informed he is the bearer of "'something exceedingly precious'" which Mr. Perry inferred must be to do with "'a *lady*'" (68)—or, for that matter, when she is detailing the comments of anyone upon a subject she has at heart.

Harriet is in fact a social creature. Emma notes her gratitude at being first received in the way she is, and the pleasure she evinces at her hostess's affability and parting handshake; and the responsiveness of a different order when, having been driven to the Martins', Harriet looks around "with a sort of fearful curiosity" before her chilling resumption of relations with them (186). The account of the meeting she gives afterwards so well conveys the naturalness and delicacy of feelings on both sides as to cause Emma alarm. But there was in truth nothing for her to fear. Harriet's protestation earlier, upon realising that Emma must have dropped acquaintance with her had she married Mr. Martin—"It would have killed me never to come to Hartfield any more!"—had expressed what was for her the true scale of values. She feels as strongly as the other the distinction which admission to that demesne has accorded her (54).

This is to be confirmed in intimate terms as Emma endeavours to check her wistful preoccupation with Mr. Elton by mention of the pain which being reminded of her error brings, and Harriet's need for her own sake to acquire the habit of proper self-command. By this hint of thanklessness on her part, Harriet is plunged into a violence of remorse.

> "You, who have been the best friend I ever had in my life—Want gratitude to you!—Nobody is equal to you! I care for nobody as I do for you! Oh, Miss Woodhouse, how ungrateful I have been!" (268)

Nothing becomes Harriet more than this display of "tenderness of heart," as Emma esteems it; nor is the latter wrong in being tempted at this point to consider the young girl as exceeding her in attractiveness. She recognises the want in herself of the capacity for affection which Harriet possesses in having an instinctive liking for people. It is in fact Harriet's social predisposition which puts an end to her tenderness for Mr. Elton. Her sense of the humiliation she is subjected to at the Crown by his ostentatious declining to dance with her is acute: as is her awareness of its dissipation by Knightley's courtly offer of his hand. The whole is an intense experience for her. "'Such a change!'" she declares afterwards to Emma; "'In one moment such a change! From perfect misery to perfect happiness'" (342). From what she had said before they quitted the ballroom Emma has realized that it was as if her

eyes were suddenly opened to Elton's character; but she does not appreciate the depth of deliverance socially speaking Knightley's intervention has
constituted for Harriet: what must be its significance for a nature as open
and sensitive as hers.

* * *

For Harriet is naturally drawn to the opposite sex; and though always
conducting herself with modesty, is not inhibited by undue reserve. There
is an appreciative regard for the gentlemen she encounters at Hartfield,
and a respect, which can amount to near-reverence, for their virtues. Mr.
Woodhouse's gentleness she had voluntarily remarked upon with admiration verging upon awe; first acquaintance with Mr. Knightley produces the
open admiration of his being "'so very fine a man!'" (32), and even when
Mr. Elton is lost to her, she can aver that it will remain a pleasure to admire
him at a distance, and "'think of his superiority to all the rest of the world
with the gratitude, wonder, and veneration which are so proper, in me
especially'" (341).

Is this responsiveness to men the explanation of Harriet's extraordinary
amatory career? If it were, it would declare her more than a little of a coquette,
and betoken an instability or shallowness of disposition making her unworthy
of being taken seriously. If, though, it is not, the question must be asked why in
the first place Emma should have found it possible to blight her protégée's early
but very real affection for young farmer Martin with little apparent difficulty.

The answer surely lies in the influence which Emma is able so clev-
erly and determinedly to exert. The slightest suggestion of an attachment
from Harriet is enough to call forth the assurance of her being a gentleman's
daughter, and consequent necessity of supporting her claim to that status "'by
every thing within your own power,'" against those intent upon lowering her,
to wit, the Martins. Their meeting with Mr. Martin next day on the Donwell
road is prelude to deliberate vilification of his appearance and manner, which
brings from Harriet the abashed admission that "'he is not so genteel as real
gentlemen.'" There follows a series of denigrating comparisons with men
of the Hartfield circle, and introduction thereupon of Mr. Elton's charms,
with allusion to the recent "'additional softness'" of address by which, "'If
he means anything, it must be to please you.'" By these means is "the very
person fixed on by Emma" now flatteringly introduced to Harriet's shaken
sensibilities (30–34).

The business of prevailing upon her to reject Martin's proposal is admi-
rably contrived. There is no urging: instead, an assumption as between ladies
of a negative in such a case being without question, of course accompanied by

"'expressions of gratitude and concern for the pain you are inflicting'"—succeeded by affected restrained surprise at the possible existence of "'doubt as to the *purport* of your answer.'" Instantly, the intention is understood. "'You think I ought to refuse him then?' said Harriet, looking down." Ensuing protestations of unwillingness to advise or influence are beside the point: the damage has been done. For her now to accept Martin, as Harriet is acutely aware, would mean the sacrifice of a unique friendship, an abandonment of all that Emma prizes in her and is yet to come to fulfillment, and a betrayal of the social convictions and aspirations that are a true component of her being (51–52).

Such loss and harm, at this early stage of her life, Harriet is not able to contemplate. It is all the more remarkable, therefore, that once decision has been reached and letter despatched, she should display residual independence of mind to the extent of contradicting to her face what Emma has so strenuously impressed on her. Certainly, she concedes, with respect to handsomeness and manner he may not equal others; "'However, I do really think Mr. Martin a very amiable young man, and have a great opinion of him'" (54). This view, here boldly stated, she can never change, under any form of persuasion, or whatever else may betide: and she confirms it the moment she has the chance.

In recommending Mr. Elton to her, Emma exerts influence of an entirely different kind. The method of disparagement with admixture of pretence, which Martin's inferior social position had made requisite, now gives place to an impulsion of the purest friendship and goodwill. Emma "had no scruple with regard to Mr. Elton," convinced as she is of his being "in the fairest way of falling in love, if not in love already" with her young charge; and while she cannot feel any doubt of having given Harriet's fancy "a proper direction" at the earliest moment by assurance of his admiration, she assiduously follows it up "by agreeable hints" (42). She goes about her task with a delighted certainty, with an enthusiasm at the near-realisation of her dream, by which Harriet, in her inexperience, and fresh from her confined upbringing, is impelled to view matters through her benefactress's eyes.

Emma's attributing Elton's attentions to a love for Harriet, gratifying though the idea be, is not a product of her active imagination. She cannot conceive of so inordinate a propensity in him as to have designs upon herself. Her action when he has presented his charade is thus fully expressive of her mind. Smilingly, she pushes the paper towards Harriet with the words, "'take it,—it is for you. Take your own.'" The word *courtship* can be no other than "'a very good hint'" of the desire to pay his addresses; and the poem's application, as Emma construes it, is so pointed and particular a compliment "'that I cannot have a moment's doubt as to Mr. Elton's intentions. You are his object—and you will soon receive the completest proof of it'" (70–73). The purpose it denotes is as clear, she assures Harriet, as her own wishes for her have been since she first knew her.

The interchange that follows is charged with Emma's exclamations and congratulations: upon the naturalness and desirability of the attachment, its being in every sense prudential and advantageous, its acceptability to friends and family, its elevating tendency, its giving every prospect of happiness through Elton's amiable character, its arising between people called together by situation, and belonging to each other '"by every circumstance of your respective homes."' The list is all but exhaustive: and the certainty is complete.

As far as Harriet is concerned, Emma speaks with a womanly and social authority that is irresistible; and yet, in the very act of yielding to it, she gives voice to intimations of a contrary sort. '"Whatever you say is always right,"' she cries; '"and therefore I suppose, and believe, and hope it must be so; but otherwise I could not have imagined it'" (74). The gradations of her acquiescence are significant—as are the reasons she puts forward for her misgiving. Elton in his eligibility is '"so much beyond anything I deserve"'; his interest in her '"is a sort of thing which nobody could have expected"'; and she '"did not know him, to speak to him, at Michaelmas!"' (75). These considerations are commonsense. From their perspective what Emma is urging is most unlikely: but Harriet is without means of resisting it. And soon she is reduced to, '"How nicely you talk; I love to hear you. You understand every thing'" (76).

That she is without defence is the fault, not of herself, but of the usages of social life that directed relations between the sexes. Attachment and wooing were on both sides a matter of suggestion—delicate, as in the bestowal of compliment, or more explicit, by such gesture or token as the conferring of Harriet's portrait on Elton, or his ceremonious presentation of the charade. By her generous invitations to Hartfield, and the easy sociability she favours him with on Harriet's account, Emma is unwittingly guilty of a liberality that Elton, and even the disinterested Mr. John Knightley, can understand only as encouragement (112). Ordinarily, however, a heedfulness alike in behaviour and in its interpretation is rigorously observed. The Eltons and Knightleys, the Wentworths and Bertrams, agonise over having their discreet inferences "understood" by the beloved: and Harriet is not the least credulous, fanciful or foolish in being guided by Emma's appraisal of the indications in Mr. Elton's conduct. There is for her, in addition, the flattering thought that, just as greatness in Emma's person has lifted her out of obscurity into distinction, so it is now coming more wonderfully to her aid, in Mr. Elton, '"who might marry any body!"' succumbing to her charms. Could someone as innocent and trusting as she be expected to oppose so felicitous a development, guarded and instructed as she is by an Emma

Woodhouse? Harriet is no simpleton in believing herself beloved by this respected gentleman, but reacts to the unusual circumstance as would any well-conducted lady of her tender years.

* * *

For Emma, strolling on Hartfield's lawns the morning after the Westons' ball, her head full of gratified musings upon Knightley's gallantry to Harriet, to be confronted with the sight of the sweep gates opening to admit the same Harriet in swooning state on Frank Churchill's arm, after his rescuing her from the gipsies, is a masterpiece of literary construction. No manner of person whatsoever, as Jane Austen mischievously affirms thereupon, would have been dead to the happening's romantic possibilities. Certainly Emma's mind is not proof against them; and afterwards it seems to her the most natural thing in the world that Harriet should be confessing an utter devotion to her champion, though with hopelessness as to the likelihood of his stooping to her. Influence, therefore, is not called for here; and Emma, chastened now as she is by recollection of the confusion and distress she had involved Harriet and herself in over Elton, is resolved against the slightest interference, even to the mention of a name. Her advice is therefore what might properly be given to any young woman in this predicament: that matches of such disparity are not altogether without precedent, and that she should observe with the closest attention the beloved's attitude towards her (342).

Harriet is of course talking about Mr. Knightley. The service he had rendered her the previous evening, in its moral and social implication, is for her infinitely greater than the physical deliverance Churchill has just effected. For the latter she is naturally obliged: but by the former she has been captivated. It would have reduced to insignificance any allure that Churchill's forthright conduct might have conferred on him; but in fact Harriet has never even thought of Churchill, except to be conscious of his lacking the distinction, the true gentlemanliness, she had recognised in Knightley. In this she has shown herself possessed of a measure of discrimination which Emma, distracted possibly by romantic schemings, is yet to attain; and at the tense moment when misunderstanding is finally rectified, it is with indignation that Harriet rejects the idea of her having been predisposed as Emma had imagined.

> "Mr. Frank Churchill, indeed! I do not know who would ever look at him in the company of the other. I hope I have a better taste than to think of Mr. Frank Churchill, who is like nobody by his side." (405)

This outspokenness is in part due to the pressure of wounded feelings; but it tends at least to demonstrate that Harriet is far from being the sentimentalist, the innate romantic, that her dealings might at first suggest.

Falling in love with Mr. Knightley is something she does entirely of her own accord. It is a love born of admiration and esteem; but it arises also from immense gratitude. Knightley's inviting her to dance upon her being scorned by Elton was more than rescue from social affront. It had in truth been a healing in emotional terms, for a nature simple and sincere, shocked and dismayed at sudden perfidy in the man for whom she had entertained a genuine affection. The restoration brought about in her manifested itself outwardly in her bounding "higher than ever" in the dance, and being "in a continual course of smiles": but its effect upon the heart has been far more dramatic, though unseen (328).

It is the greater for what is not present in Harriet's awareness. She has no means of comprehending Elton's ill-treatment to have been a revenge upon Emma for the insult she had administered in specifying his social inferiority, both in the match she had sought to contrive, and that to which he had himself aspired. Quite what sense she might have gained of Knightley's acting to quell a flagrant discourtesy, and in preservation of social decorum, would be hard to determine. But his deepest motive—a wish to remedy the injury to Emma in this public slighting of her friend, an impulse of love itself, which escaped Emma's own recognition—Harriet could not begin to fathom.

As any young woman might, she views what has happened from a personal perspective: sees herself singled out, honoured, redeemed by the man she has throughout identified as in a class apart from the others. His asking for her hand in that situation was the highest compliment that could be paid within the sphere of her experience. With this certainty, enhanced as it is by powerful feelings of thankfulness, she cannot doubt herself as being the woman preferred—and as yet again distinguished by a benign suzerainty seemingly intent on claiming her as its own.

That his inviting her to the dance might be liable to such interpretation would not occur to Knightley. From his social altitude he would, like Emma, never expect persons admitted to a modicum of familiarity to venture above their condition, presuming upon an invulnerability which, however, in the nature of things, a moment's inadvertence might dispel. What preoccupies him is a desire to defend his Emma against affront, and thereby perhaps re-establish himself in her goodwill by graciousness towards a girl he has without doubt judged too severely in the past. The particularity implicit in his so doing can but be regarded, by Harriet and onlookers alike, as a marked attention. The incident, with all that subsequently flows from it in Knightley's seeking with the same determination to cultivate further acquaintance with her, has the appearance in ordinary social terms—as ultimately to Emma's own understanding—of plain romantic attachment.

Harriet is therefore justified in the hopes of Knightley which, in discourse somewhat hesitant and by no means "[m]ethodical, or well arranged" (409), she is later to confide to her sponsor. Bearing in mind the vulnerability with which she is beset by reason of her few years and scant experience, and the pressures social and emotional so arbitrarily brought to bear upon her at Hartfield, her having been or fancied herself in love with him, as with Elton, is in the light of events not at all as remarkable as would appear. And when, freed at last from the affliction of Emma's tutelage, she chances to re-encounter Martin in London, she gives evidence of a praiseworthy maturity, both in the constancy of her first love despite the onslaught made against it, and in the decisiveness she demonstrates in there and then accepting him.

* * *

When Fanny Price comes to live at Mansfield Park, the Bertram girls are unremitting in their disparagement of their poor cousin for her inferiority. The one respect in which they will allow her any equality with them is disclosed in the grudging admission that "'Fanny is good-natured enough.'" This attribute is largely to be seen in Fanny's compliance with the obligations of her dependent situation at Mansfield, and a readiness to be generally helpful: but with Harriet Smith, it is evident in a variety of relationships in Highbury and at Hartfield. It is perhaps at its most moving in her reception of the news of Emma's having been in error as to Elton's feelings and intentions. There is no blame, no recrimination; instead, a "lowly opinion of herself" which acquits the other of accountability. The affection of such a man, she protests amidst her tears, would have been "'too great a distinction.'" She never could have merited it; indeed, "'nobody but so partial and kind a friend as Miss Woodhouse would have thought it possible'" (141–42). Both he and the as yet unknown Miss Hawkins are held in high regard: and merely to reflect that he had not thrown himself away is for Harriet "'such a comfort!'" (272).

Almost as affecting is the sensitivity and the tenderness that is demonstrated during her accidental encounter with Mr. Martin and his sister at Ford's, after relationship with them has been abruptly ended. She is near fainting, knowing that she will have turned as white as her gown. In the sister's coming forward and seeming ready to shake hands, Harriet is sorely conscious of the reluctance Elizabeth has contrived to overcome. Her state is not so much embarrassment, as misery at the couple's struggling to hide their

pain in complaisance; and Elizabeth's expression of regret at their not meeting now is "'almost too kind'" for her to bear (179).

But it is surely in her unfailing amiability towards Emma that Harriet's
good nature is most apparent. Not only has she repeatedly been led into disap-
pointment and grief, but the friend whose self-centred enthusiasms have been
responsible is unmasked at the close as an enemy. Yet so unassuming, gentle
and mannerly has she been in all, that not the least semblance of reproach has
passed her lips or appeared in her reactions. After Harriet is banished from
Hartfield to the John Knightleys in London, Emma can fancy there being
present in her letters "something of resentment, a something bordering on it
in her style," which, she realises, "might be only her own consciousness"—or
in other words, the trick of a merited self-reproach. But even if the former, as
she goes on to tell herself, "it seemed as if an angel only could have been quite
without resentment under such a stroke" as her appropriation of Knightley.
Having, in short, consistently been made a fool of in concerns close to the
heart, Harriet reveals, in disposition and in conduct, qualities which by any
standard must be seen as admirable (451).

* * *

Amongst them is one which her naiveté and want of cultivation might lead
us not to expect. It is to be detected in the conversation with Emma that
follows their encountering Mr. Martin. When the mistress of Hartfield,
describing him as awkward and abrupt, asks with rhetorical emphasis what
he will be at Mr. Weston's time of life, Harriet responds with a solemn,
"'There is no saying, indeed!'"; and the answer of Emma's own providing,
that he will have become "'a completely gross, vulgar farmer,'" receives
the quiet accord of "'Will he, indeed, that will be very bad'" (33). Even
allowing for Harriet's inclination and habit of respectfulness, there is, in
her demeanour as she meets this slander of the man in whose company
she had experienced much pleasure, a deliberative reticence that merits the
name of composure.

It is evident also when, under Emma's reproof as to her being "'over-
powered'" by so small a token of admiration as Mr. Elton's charade, she
replies with the brevity and self-possession of "'Oh! no—I hope I shall not
be ridiculous about it. Do as you please'" (77–78). The same tones accompany
her appearance before Emma one morning with the Tunbridge-ware box,
and confession of having treasured Elton's relics therein. Now professedly
an altered creature, she declares a duty and wish to have no reserves from
Emma on the subject; and continues, "'it is very fit that you should have the
satisfaction of knowing it. I do not want to say any more than is necessary—I

am too much ashamed of having given way as I have done, and I dare say you understand me'" (337). The matter itself is trivial: but the language by which it is conveyed, in its simplicity, has an elegance of its own.

More often than not, the mode of speech mirrors the mind of the speaker. What, therefore, are we to make of Harriet's words at the moment when realisation has dawned upon Emma that it is Mr. Knightley, and not Frank Churchill, for whom her friend has been nurturing so passionate a regard? "'I am sure, but for believing that you entirely approved and meant to encourage me in my attachment,'" she protests, "'I should have considered it at first too great a presumption almost, to dare to think of him'" (405–06). That a degree of sophistication rings through these accents is borne out by the style and content of what ensues. Emma, exclaiming at the "'most unfortunate—most deplorable mistake!'" (407) she has made, is reduced to silence. Its significance is not lost upon Harriet, and she responds with an injunction whose mild terms in no way belie its directness. The possibility of such a match has been Emma's own urging: and "'if Mr. Knightley should really—if *he* does not mind the disparity, I hope, dear Miss Woodhouse, you will not set yourself against it, and try to put difficulties in the way. But you are too good for that, I am sure.'"

Her meaning could hardly be more plain, yet it is not offensive. Perhaps its very clarity takes any hurtfulness from it: but this can only be when the disposition behind the utterance is innocent and engaging. Of its being so with Harriet, if it were not evident from her previous attitudes, there would be confirmation in her final remark. Until this point, she declares, she had as instructed gone by outward indications of regard in Knightley: "'But now I seem to feel that I may deserve him; and that if he does choose me, it will not be any thing so very wonderful'" (411). In this speech there is a confidence and womanliness which impresses—and conveys the truth that Harriet has about her at this testing juncture an innate dignity, which others, of more years and greater claim, might well envy.

* * *

But does Harriet have the stature which might make some future Austen heroine? The comparison suggests itself with Catherine Morland, who is also at the stage between girl and woman, and certainly not a giant of intellect—but who displays an adherence to principle, a resolution in the face of difficulties, and an ability to think something through which can unsettle even a Henry Tilney. But Catherine has not been subjected to another's authority—save that of Mrs. Allen, which for all practical purposes can be safely discounted. She is obliged almost throughout to stand on her own feet, whereas Harriet, confined to a subordinate role, has small scope for initiative; were she placed in a similar situation, indications are that she would acquit herself creditably. In Fanny Price, by contrast, we observe a profoundly moral nature and contingent strength of personality that can slowly impress itself upon wholly adverse circumstances. But the demands of everyday living oblige her to withdraw into a diffidence which masks her superiority from all who do not know her well; and the hesitation and solemnity of manner which results robs her, in the opinion of many, of heroic pretension.

How different is Harriet's refreshing spontaneity and naturalness. Certainly there is little in her outlook of a detached and speculative kind: her thoughts are a process of responses to events around her, and the hopes, joys and sorrows they give rise to. But the same can largely be said of all Jane Austen's young women: none of them is the stuff philosophers are made of. They are in love with the present as they encounter it, with the men they will marry, when they have found them; and do not seem at the point we know them to be seeking much beyond.

However, there is an exception to what has just been said that concerns Harriet. It has to do with a remark she makes at the end of her account of the distressing meeting with Martin and his sister at Ford's, from which the rain permitted no escape. She would rather have done anything, she tells Emma, than have had it happen: "'and yet, you know, there was a sort of satisfaction in seeing him behave so pleasantly and kindly. And Elizabeth, too'" (179). In the midst of her anguish at such close contact after the estrangement, she has been struck by the rightness of conduct and delicacy of sentiment in those now permanently distanced from her. Her being so is a piece of wonderment and true reflection. But it is more.

If what defines a gentleman is his predominant desire to set others at their ease, may it not be that a corresponding pleasure in fineness of comportment, and the decencies of social interplay, is what distinguishes a lady? If this be allowed—and who would pronounce otherwise?—it suggests, with much else, that, deceived though Emma may sometimes have been as to character and conduct in the unfolding of events, she made no mistake in her choice of Harriet Smith.

JULIET MCMASTER

Emma: *The Geography of a Mind*

Let me start with that wonderful passage near the center of the novel, where Emma observes the street scene in Highbury. For her it is a moment of still water, as it were, between the Harriet–Elton debacle and the Frank–Jane affair; between the dinner at the Coles and the visit to hear Jane Fairfax play on her new piano. Here we see Emma briefly at leisure, waiting outside Ford's shop while Harriet dithers over a purchase, and we learn something of Highbury as a community:

> Much could not he hoped from the traffic of even the busiest part
> of Highbury; . . . and when her eyes fell only on the butcher with
> his tray, a tidy old woman travelling homewards from shop with
> her full basket, two curs quarrelling over a dirty bone, and a string
> of dawdling children round the baker's little bow-window eyeing
> the gingerbread, she knew she had no reason to complain, and was
> amused enough. . . . A mind lively and at ease, can do with seeing
> nothing, and can see nothing that does not answer. (233)

Emma's mind, we know, is always "lively," but not so often "at ease." But for now she is well entertained. Her mind can "do with seeing nothing"—nothing of major import, that is, or nothing she needs to take over the management

From *Persuasions* 29 (2007): 26–38. © 2007 by Juliet McMaster.

of; and it "can see nothing that does not answer"—for her present purpose of being amused. We could explore the last phrase further: Emma's hyperactive mind, with her habit of eager over-interpretation, can always make something out of nothing. Making something out of nothing, some might claim, is an activity we see her busy at throughout the novel. "The mind is its own place," wrote Milton, in a wonderfully resonant passage:

> The mind is its own place, and in itself
> Can make a Heaven of Hell, a Hell of Heaven.
>   (*Paradise Lost* 1.254–55)

Of course Milton isn't the only writer who has envisaged the mind spatially, as a place where things happen, as a space populated by ideas and stocked with furniture, as a country with its own government and physical features. "My mind to me a kingdom is," wrote Edward Dyer—the most memorable line he ever penned. Jane Austen's favorite poet Cowper suggests social geography when he writes of "His mind his kingdom and his will his law"—endowing the mind with a political constitution and a legal system. Gerard Manley Hopkins invokes physical geography when he exclaims, "O the mind, mind has mountains, / Cliffs of fall. . . ." Wordsworth sends the mind to sea when he contemplates Newton's "mind for ever / Voyaging through strange seas of thought alone."[1] Milton's Belial, a fiend in hell who might well choose annihilation, nevertheless clings to the life of the mind, a place that extends all limitations:

> For who would lose,
> Though full of pain, this intellectual being,
> Those thoughts that wander through eternity?
>   (*Paradise Lost* 2.146–48)

Of an entity so complex, so incomprehensible as the human mind, we feel the need to provide "a local habitation and a name," to envisage it as something familiar and definable: a country, a mansion, a castle in a landscape. Nineteenth-century phrenologists mapped the brain, assigning physical locations, or bumps on the skull, to such mental attributes as conscience and benevolence. Freud too had to people the mind with *dramatis personae*, the godlike Superego, the everyman Ego, the lurking subterranean Id—reminding us of the mediaeval stage set-up, with an upper floor for God and his angels, a middle stage for the human drama, a pit below for the devil and all his demons.

Such figurings of the mind often expand to allegory, as the human psyche becomes the field of action in which conflicting principles do battle.

"Let me be nothing," declares Sir Thomas Browne, who may be called the first autobiographer, "if within the compass of my self I find not the battail of Lepanto, Passion against Reason, Reason against Faith, Faith against the Devil, and my Conscience against all" (Browne 96). That wide compass of the Self provides a field for the exploration of the human spirit. Allegory as a form, so natural a means of exploring the mind in the Renaissance, may seem quaint and outmoded in the twenty-first century. But I suggest to you that it is a mode not altogether alien to Austen, even though she is first and foremost a writer of realistic fiction. The wide compass of the Self, and the intricate operation of the mind, is indeed her territory.

Is the novel *Emma* an allegory, then? I certainly wouldn't claim so much. But I suggest that parts of it can be read allegorically, and that a somewhat allegorical reading will lead us to places in Emma's mind that we want to take note of. We've all noticed that Mr. Knightley lives at Done-Well Abbey, and that Emma the matchmaker lives in the Field of the Heart, Hartfield. And Austen uses those abstract nouns of mental attributes—such terms as *temper*, *imagination*, *fancy*, *conscience*—with the kind of precision and fine discrimination that belongs to allegory. Sometimes she even introduces her own little fleeting mini-allegories. After the ball at the Crown, Mr. Knightley guesses that Emma had tried to match Elton with Harriet, and she admits he is right:

> "I shall not scold you [he smiles indulgently]. I leave you to your own reflections."
>
> "Can you trust me with such flatterers?—Does nay vain spirit ever tell me I am wrong?"
>
> "Not your vain spirit, but your serious spirit.—If one leads you wrong, I am sure the other tells you of it." (330)

Momentarily we view Emma as holding court among her own mental attributes, her reflections as flatterers, her vain spirit congratulating her for her behavior, her serious spirit reminding her of her errors—like Doctor Faustus beset by his Good Angel and Evil Angel. And in fact Mr. Knightley himself recurrently enacts the role of Emma's "serious spirit"—"'proving [him]self [her] friend by very faithful counsel'" when her vain spirit leads her wrong (375).

As an analogy, let me remind you of a classic allegory that Austen is very likely to have known, Edmund Spenser's *The Faerie Queene*.[2] In Canto 9 of Book Two, Spenser embeds an allegory of the human body and the human mind in the larger allegory that is the poem as a whole. Sir Guyon, the Knight of Temperance, visits a castle that is run by Alma, the Soul. The castle represents the body: the mouth becomes the gate, the stomach a cauldron, the lungs a huge bellows, the heart a parlor where Cupid plays, and so on. But the part that concerns me is the "stately turret," the mind, which is lit by two beacons, the eyes. Here in the mind dwell Alma's three sage counselors: one, the first and youngest, tells Alma of things to come; the second advises her on the present; the third and oldest records the past. We can call them Imagination, Judgment, and Memory.

Imagination doesn't come off very well in Spenser's allegory. His chamber is decorated with mythological beasts and monsters, and filled with buzzing flies:

> All those were idle thoughts and fantasies,
> Devices, dreames, opinions unsound . . .
> And all that fained is, as leasings, tales, and lies. (2.9.51)

We could consider this as a hostile view of Emma in her "state of schemes, and hopes, and connivance" (343). Emma is the "imaginist" and "'great dreamer'" (335, 345).

The second sage, Judgment, fares much better. He is "a man of ripe and perfect age, . . . goodly reason and grave personage"; and in his chamber are pictures "Of Magistrates, of courts, of tribunals . . . / Of lawes, of judgements" (2.9.54, 53): surely a model for Mr. Knightley, the magistrate!

And what of the third sage, Memory, described as "an old oldman, halfe blind, / And all decrepit in his feeble corse" (2.9.55)? Mr. Woodhouse, shall we say? But I don't want to labor the analogy.

It's revealing, I think, to envisage Emma's mind as a place. We as readers certainly spend a lot of time there, seeing what she sees, interpreting as she interprets (until we learn better), responding as she does to what feel like changes in the weather: little gusts of passion, moments of damp discomfort when she is out of sympathy with Mr. Knightley, gleams of delight at fair prospects. Though as informed readers, on the dozenth reading of the novel, we may be able to stand back, looking *at* Emma from outside her, and recognize how terribly she is blundering, and shake our fingers at her in reproof, I ask you for a moment to suspend judgment and look about you. Here we are, tourists in Emma's mind. Let's check out the scenery. "'[V]ouchsafe to let your imagination wander,'" as she tells Mr. Knightley (350).

It is not a crowded place. Human company is rather scarce, in fact, for there are few people admitted to genuine intimacy. On the departure of Miss Taylor—and there are many reasons for the novel's beginning at that first deprivation of Emma's experience—she is now "in great danger . . . , of intellectual solitude," we hear, for her father is "no companion for her" (7). For all her vigorous social activity, at the outset Emma is lonely in the mind. She needs to fill the empty spaces with activity, projects, connivings.

Nevertheless, here in Emma's mind we find ourselves in a sunny land, bright, healthy, prosperous. We might see her mind like the grounds of Donwell Abbey, "sweet to the eye and the mind. English verdure . . . seen under a sun bright, without being oppressive" (360). (I'll come back later to the sun in Emma's mind.) Despite her father's and sister's obsession with ailments, Emma is never ill; she is in fact "'the picture of health'" (39). No disasters have scourged this land, no earthquakes or floods have scarred it or laid it waste. At age twenty-one, apart from the loss of her mother, which she does not remember, she has had "very little to distress or vex her" (5). Imagine how happy and pleasant that life must be in which your first conscious sorrow has been the marriage and removal—and not very far at that—of your best friend. Only that is the event that has "first brought grief" (6). And the sunshine and good cheer of Emma's mind are not just a passive contentment, but an active and conscious condition. We often see Emma looking about her at her situation, taking stock, and congratulating herself on the pleasant prospect: "Harriet rational, Frank Churchill not too much in love, and Mr. Knightley not wanting to quarrel with her, how very happy a summer must be before her!" (332).

This country of Emma's mind is a very *busy* place, too. A lot is going on, and very briskly. When Emma watches that tidy old woman with her basket, and the dawdling children eyeing the gingerbread at the baker's, she is on the threshold of making a story about them. And in the case of the people closer to her, she does make the story about them, and she takes energetic steps to make the story happen. If her thoughts don't "wander through eternity," in Milton's haunting phrase, they are much more active and purposeful. The thoughts that people her mind are marshaled into action. Mr. Knightley imagines her

> "saying to [her]self one idle day, 'I think it would be a very good thing for Miss Taylor if Mr. Weston were to marry her.'"

But Emma's days are seldom idle. Her body may be at leisure, but the thought is spurred to vigorous performance. As she claims proudly, she "'promoted Mr. Weston's visits here, and [gave] many little encouragements, and smoothed many little matters'"; and her efforts are crowned with "success" (12–13). In this novel, the action that counts happens in the mind. As my lost friend and colleague Bruce Stovel wrote, "the primary change . . . is internal."[3]

Inside Emma's mind, things are going on all the time, and very fast. Amid her father's desultory maunderings, and the "quiet prosings" of Mrs.

Goddard and Mrs. and Miss Bates, Emma as hostess is alert: "With an alacrity beyond the common impulse of a spirit which yet was never indifferent to the credit of doing every thing well and attentively, with the real goodwill of a mind delighted with its own ideas, did she then do all the honours of the meal" (22, 24). "Alacrity" is typical of Emma's mental operations. With "the rapidity of half a moment's thought" she translates the news of Frank Churchill's arrival into an alleviation of Harriet's love pangs (188). "It darted through her, with the speed of an arrow, that Mr. Knightley must marry no one but herself" (408). In the crucial proposal scene near the end of the novel, "with all the wonderful velocity of thought" (430), Emma is able to comprehend a whole new landscape around her: that Mr. Knightley is not in love with Harriet; that he is in love with her; that he has believed her in love with Frank Churchill; and that she had better find a way to accept him without sounding too wildly inconsistent. With alacrity, rapidity, velocity, the speed of an arrow: that's the way things move in the country of this mind.

And Emma is stimulatingly aware of her own mental operations; she spends time in the mind, rearranging the furniture, as it were, or tending the garden. She often takes mental stock, for instance of Harriet's state of heart: "[h]aving arranged all these matters, looked them through, and put them all to rights," she returns with spirits refreshed to the demands of her nephews and her father (332). Seeing Mr. Knightley approaching her in the shrubbery, when she had thought him sixteen miles away, she has "time only for the quickest arrangement of mind" (424). And she is able to pull off the rearrangement of mind without dropping a stitch (to mix the metaphor)!

I want to remind you how invigorating it is to be in a mind so active, supple, suggestive, rapid. Yes, we know how seriously Emma can go wrong; we are privy to her most embarrassing and most damaging mistakes. But this location in a mind delighted with its own ideas, this power of tracking the wonderful velocity of thought, these are the privileges that make us return to re-read the novel with fresh delight, time after time.

And as we look around ourselves in this kingdom that is Emma's mind, we can also recognize that it's a place where the government may not always be just or wise, but it will be thorough and self-regarding, and the records will be kept scrupulously up-to-date. At one point, advising Harriet in a crisis, Emma reflects, "[I]t would be safer for both, to have the judicious law of her own brain laid down with speed" (341)—and it's amusing to find her recognizing that she does lay down the law, for Harriet as well as herself. But she polices her own operations, and honestly keeps tally. After the Elton disaster, she finds herself "obliged in common honesty to stop and admit that her own behaviour to him had been . . . complaisant" (136). When she undergoes the painful process of enlightenment, she is quick to blame herself for her "insufferable vanity" in having "believed herself in the secret of everybody's feelings" (412–13)—trespassing in the minds of others, that is; and she blames herself accordingly, and makes it her business "[t]o understand, thoroughly understand her own heart" (412). (It is typical of Emma that she has to bring her brain to bear on the analysis of her heart.) And in her strenuous effort to recognize her own errors, she contrasts with that other fortunate, happy spirit, Frank Churchill. When he considers whether he had any right to bind Jane Fairfax in a secret engagement, he writes breezily: "'For my temptation to *think* it a right, I refer every caviller to a brick house ... in Highbury'" where Jane lives (437); that is, he cheerfully assumes that his love justifies his deceptions. Emma is much more exacting in the moral standards that she applies to herself.

In this busy, sunny, fully-regulated land that is Emma's mind, can we distinguish features in the landscape? Let's call the Imagination a cloud-capped mountain: for the tourist-reader the most prominent scenic feature, and for Emma herself an eminence from which she can descry and predict the busy activities of her neighbors. Johnson defines Imagination as "the power of forming ideal pictures; the power of representing things absent to one's self or others." "Ideal pictures" for Johnson relates to the Platonic Idea, which is more real than the passing images of it that we encounter in our transient lives. "The power of representing things absent to one's self or others," the creative power of the poet, is likewise positively viewed, for the "things absent" have their own reality. Emma's imagination is among her strengths, even if it can also lead her wrong. It is her "imagination" that produces the belief that Jane Fairfax is in love with Mr. Dixon (168). And when she imagines that Mr. Elton is in love with Harriet, she does serious damage, and makes a resolution of "repressing imagination all the rest of her life" (142). But it is also her imagination that creates her sympathy for Jane Fairfax in her governess troubles and enables her sympathy for Harriet.

Moreover, Emma is able to observe her own imaginings, and to learn from them. When she has imagined herself in love with Frank, she moves into novelist's mode, "forming a thousand amusing schemes for the progress and close of their attachment, fancying interesting dialogues, and inventing elegant letters" (264). Having created this elaborate mental fiction, she can nevertheless stand back and judge the effect: "[t]he conclusion of every imaginary declaration on his side was that she *refused him*" (264). So we have, within the large fabric of Jane Austen's fiction, this mini-romance, complete with letters and dialogue and declaration. And from the outcome of this little fiction she invents, Emma is able to learn the real state of her feelings—that she is not in fact very far gone in love with Frank Churchill. Imagination fares much better here, for all Emma's faults, than in the future-searching sage of

Spenser's allegory, with his "Devices, dreames, [and] opinions unsound." For Emma, imagination can be a means of discovering the truth.

What shall we do with "[t]hat very dear part of Emma, her fancy" (214)? I shall call it her garden, which she cultivates with devotion, elaborating it with bowers, arbors, trellises and fountains, and introducing rare and exotic blooms! Remember when Mr. Weston withholds the disturbing information concerning Frank's engagement: "Her fancy was very active. Half a dozen natural children, perhaps—and poor Frank cut off!" (393). Her fancy is fertile indeed!

The distinction between imagination and fancy has occupied bigger brains than mine. But Shakespeare is a help.

> Tell me where is fancy bred,
> Or in the heart or in the head?

runs a song in *The Merchant of Venice* (3.2.63–64). Emma's fancies are indeed a product of the mind, but they pertain to the heart, as they typically relate to love and romance. Let's pause for a moment, and watch her fancy at work. Frank Churchill has just delivered a scared Harriet back to Hartfield after her encounter with the gipsies.

> Such an adventure as this,—a fine young man and a lovely young woman thrown together in such a way, could hardly fail of suggesting certain ideas to the coldest heart and the steadiest brain. So Emma thought, at least. [For a moment we are outside of Emma's mind and looking dispassionately at it with an enlightened author; but we're soon back inside.] Could a linguist, could a grammarian, could even a mathematician have seen what she did, have witnessed their appearance together, and heard their history of it, without feeling that circumstances had been at work to make them peculiarly interesting to each other?—How much more must an imaginist, like herself, be on fire with speculation and foresight!—especially with such a ground-work of anticipation as her mind had already made. (334–35)

It is engaging to watch Emma, who thinks herself so cautious after her previous errors, taking off with such confidence on her next flight of fancy.

First she reclassifies the incident as "an adventure," thus wrapping it in literary associations. Then she invests the personnel of the story with an aura of romance: no longer "Frank Churchill" and "Harriet," but "a fine young man and a lovely young woman." Next she justifies her construction of events by invoking "the coldest heart and the steadiest brain" (Where is fancy bred? In the heart or in the head?): even they could not fail to be moved by the fateful "throw[ing] together" of this hero and heroine. Now she marshals a hierarchy of the dullest, most down-to-earth and coldly unimaginative thinkers: a linguist, a grammarian, "even a mathematician"!—even such plodders could not have witnessed the scene without concluding that the couple must have become "peculiarly interesting to each other." And if these conveniently imagined unimaginative beings are convinced, *of course* she is right to be convinced too. Emma has rounded up the opposition, all those least likely to agree with her—linguists, grammarians, mathematicians, and all—and brought them all over to vote on her side.

She has created her own little allegory to justify herself in leaping to a conclusion. Now she can proclaim her own title with pride rather than humility: "how much more must an imaginist, like herself, be on fire with speculation and foresight!" Notice that "must." She convinces herself there can be no other outcome. And notice too how quickly "imagination"—the possible reality—moves to "foresight"—the foreknowledge of something actual. By such means does Emma the imaginist convince herself that her imaginings must be true.

As she continues in this line of belief, Austen offers us reminders of how limited Emma's knowledge actually is. The coincidence of Frank's being there at just the right moment has to be a stroke of Fate: "It certainly was very extraordinary!—And knowing, as she did, the favourable state of mind of each at this period, it struck her the more" (335). Wait a minute! "[K]nowing, as she did, the favourable state of mind of each at this period"? Let's remind ourselves just how much, or how little, she does know. She believes Harriet has just got over Elton, Mr. Wrong, and is in just the right state of mind to fall for Mr. Right; and that Frank needs to get over *her*, Emma, and finding Miss Right in such circumstances will do the trick. *We* know better: Harriet has just fallen for Mr. Knightley when he rescued her at the dance, and Frank is already deeply in love and even engaged to someone else altogether. And yet Emma's fanciful imaginings have such an air of plausibility, as we sit in her mind looking about us, that we are in danger of being convinced all over again. "It was not possible that the occurrence should not be strongly recommending each to the other," she concludes (335). Note the use of the double negative as a means of convincing herself: she doesn't tell herself, "It was possible they might be in love," but "It was not possible that they should *not* be in love." These are the operations of fancy and imagination in Emma's highly suggestible mind.

There's an enjoyable appropriateness to the end of this chapter, where we hear that "the story of Harriet and the gipsies" has become a favorite yarn for Emma's young nephews, who clamor for her to tell it to them, word for word, every day. J. K. Rowling, move over!

I will pause over one more mental operation: "interest." It is a word that has to a large extent lost its force with us: we may consider "interest" as not much more than mild curiosity. But in *Emma* "Interest" is where the heart is: it is home. When you are *interested* in someone, in some sense you identify with her. When Emma is moved to compassion for Jane Fairfax's suffering, she is "most sincerely interested" (379)—and the "sincerely" shows that her self is really engaged with the other. Frank Churchill professes himself "to have always felt the sort of interest in the country which none but one's own country gives" (191). To use the spatial terms I have adopted, the person in whom you are "interested" dwells in your mind; in a sense she becomes part of you.

Egoist that she is, however, Emma most rejoices in occupying other people's minds. You may consider that she virtually colonizes Harriet's mind, taking over her loves and opinions. Miss Taylor was a warmly appreciated friend because she was "knowing [in] all the ways of the family, interested in all its concerns, and peculiarly interested in herself, in every pleasure, every scheme of her's" (6). Frank's letter, "[a]s soon as she came to her own name. . . . was irresistible; every line relating to herself was interesting" (444). Emma loves to be the center of other people's universes, as she is of her own.

When Emma has her awakening, and recognizes her love for Mr. Knightley, the discovery takes the form of her realizing "how much of her happiness depended on being *first* with Mr. Knightley, first in interest and affection" (415). Subconsciously, she sees herself enthroned in his mind, just as (she discovers) he is enthroned in hers. And here, very late in the novel, we learn the secret of Emma's high spirits and active happiness, the reason that her own mind is the sunny and prosperous place it is. "Satisfied that it was so"—that is, that she *has* always been "first in ['his'] interest and affection"—she has lived that fortunate and blessed existence of which she is so happily conscious. Like Donwell Abbey, she has flourished under "a sun bright, without being oppressive" (360). *All along* her mind has basked and grown verdant in the sunshine of his attention, his warming interest that is so short a step from love.

When she believes that Mr. Knightley loves Harriet, then, that sunny fertile land at last feels the blast of a devastating storm. "[H]er mind was in all the perturbation that such a developement of self, such a burst of threatening evil, such a confusion of sudden and perplexing emotions, must create" (409). It's an ecological disaster, like a tsunami, or a blotting out of the sun that will wither the land. And she contemplates a future from which the sustaining light and warmth have been withdrawn. "The prospect before her now, was threatening to a degree that could not be entirely dispelled—that might not be even partially brightened. . . . Hartfield must be comparatively deserted; and she left to cheer her father with the spirits only of ruined happiness" (422). Emma's prospect is of a waste land. And in the best manner of allegory, the internal storm is echoed by the actual weather, as "'a cold stormy rain set in,'" and July dresses itself as December (421). She faces the withdrawal of sunshine that has for so long been so salient an influence on the health and vitality of her mind.

But this is romantic comedy, after all, not a bitter investigation of the disintegration of faith and creativity like Eliot's *The Waste Land*. Though briefly faced with the devastating possibility of the withdrawal of Mr. Knightley's interest and affection, Emma is soon reassured of its steady continuity. But the threatened storm has indeed left her "more rational, [and] more acquainted with herself" (423). Hartfield, the Field of the Heart, will be governed more wisely and rationally now.

To return to my initial quotation from Milton:

The mind is its own place, and in itself
Can make a Heaven of Hell, a Hell of Heaven.

It is an exciting proposition, and we feel that it applies to Emma too. She too can live an exciting life in this place we call the mind; she too can create beautiful fictions and believe in them. And we have all experienced the delight of dwelling in that lively place that is Emma's mind, and the invigorating belief that her mind is self-sufficient. But Milton's lines, let me remind you, are spoken by Satan. And though Satan does work hard at making a Heaven of Hell, he succeeds only in creating a diabolical inversion of Heaven. Similarly, Emma's dreams and schemes, so beguiling and so plausible, not only fail, but do damage. As with everything in Jane Austen, it's a matter of a fine balance. Yes, with Emma we enjoy being located in a mind delighted with its own ideas. But we too need reminding that Emma's mind, for all her facility in creating something out of nothing, and seeing nothing that does not answer, is not self-sufficient and omnipotent.

Can one connect the figurative geography of Emma's mind with the literal geography in the novel? I think so.

That "mind lively and at ease" that we find so congenial a location has its severe limitations. Austen knows that you don't have to travel widely to gather the experience that matters. "Provincial" was never a bad concept for her. She is rather scornful of Frank Churchill's restless desire to go to "'Swisserland'" (365), which is clearly only an expression of his dissatisfaction with his current lot. But the mind which can find so much that is entertaining in a quiet street scene in Highbury deserves further stimulation. Emma doesn't yearn, like Tennyson's Ulysses,

To follow knowledge like a sinking star,
Beyond the utmost bound of human thought.
("Ulysses" 31–32)

But in her state of "intellectual solitude" she does need and deserve company more stimulating than her father's; and she does need and deserve horizons wider than those in Highbury, or even Box Hill. In the hypochondriac talk between her father and her sister, Mr. Woodhouse denounces the John Knightleys' trip to South End and insists that "'the sea is rarely of use to any body'"—a peculiarly closed-minded position. Emma interjects, "'I must beg you not to talk of the sea. It makes me envious and miserable;—I who have never seen it!'" (101). At the time she is acting the good hostess and avoiding a quarrel. But the cry rings true. Never to have seen the sea is indeed a deprivation to her. For all her gregarious nature and social activity, there are moments when she feels the need to expand her mind by wider prospects. After the tense and unsatisfactory sociabilities of the Box Hill outing, she wishes she were "sitting almost alone, and quite unattended to, in tranquil observation of the beautiful views beneath her" (374). She would enjoy the experience that is available to Anne Elliot, who at Lyme can find "the happiest spot for watching the flow of the tide, for sitting in unwearied contemplation . . . [of] green chasms between romantic rocks" (*Persuasion* 95). The sea represents change and passionate fulfillment—Frank Churchill and Jane Fairfax fall in love at Weymouth. But given her father's intransigent position, Emma while single is unlikely to see the sea. The man who fears a half-mile carriage ride to Randalls isn't likely to take her anywhere more remote, let alone to the health-threatening seaside.

I like to think that Emma's excessive fantasizing, her busy-bodying and restless management of other people's lives, are to some extent an expression of a sense of confinement. Her mind must be active, and if she can't turn her attention to the wider scene of nature and humanity, she must get busily to work on what's going on in the minds and hearts of her immediate neighbors. When Mr. Knightley moves into the Field of the Heart, Emma will suffer no more from "intellectual solitude" (7). Moreover, as you will all remember, their marriage is immediately followed by a "fortnight's absence in a tour to the sea-side" (483). Hooray! That interior landscape that is Emma's mind is to be refreshed by sea breezes, and expanded to new and far horizons. And we who are gathered here by the great Pacific, like Emma herself, can rejoice in our own access of knowledge, and our own widening horizons.

Notes

1. I here cluster the references for my brief quotations: Edward Dyer, the lyric beginning with this line; William Cowper, "Truth"; Gerard Manley Hopkins, the sonnet beginning "No worst, there is none"; William Wordsworth, *The Prelude* 3.63–64.

2. Her brother James Austen owned a 1758 edition of *The Faerie Queene*, which may well have come from her father's library of 500 books that seem to have

been sold to James when his parents and sisters moved to Bath in 1801. See Gilson (433,435). I am grateful to Susan Allen Ford, editor of *Persuasions*, for alerting me to this connection.

3. Bruce Stovel's paper, published in *New Windows on a Woman's World*, was read at this conference in lieu of the paper he would have given but for his untimely death on January 12, 2007.

WORKS CITED

Austen, Jane. *The Novels of Jane Austen*. Ed. R.W. Chapman. 3rd ed. Oxford: OUP, 1933–69.

Browne, Sir Thomas. *Religio Medici. The Works of Sir Thomas Browne*. Ed. Charles Soyle. Vol. 1. Edinburgh: Grant, 1912. 7–112.

Gilson, David. *A Bibliography of Jane Austen*. New Castle, DE: Oak Knoll, 1977.

Johnson, Samuel. *A Dictionary of the English Language*. 2 vols. London, 1822.

Stovel, Bruce. "The New Emma in *Emma*." *New Windows on a Woman's World: Essays for Jocelyn Harris*. Ed. Colin Gibson and Lisa Marr. Vol. 2. Dunedin, NZ: Department of English, University of Otago, 2005. 104–15. Rpt. in *Persuasions On-Line* 28.1 (2007).

LAURA MOONEYHAM WHITE

Beyond the Romantic Gypsy: Narrative Disruptions and Ironies in Austen's Emma

I was stolen by the gypsies.
My parents stole me right back. Then
the gypsies stole me again.
This went on for a long time.

—Charles Simic, "I Was Stolen by the Gypsies"

As this epigraph from Simic suggests, stories about gypsies have a very long and murky history. The history of the actual Romany people is almost as obscure. It seems that they entered France in the early fifteenth century and Great Britain gradually in the sixteenth century following their expulsion from Spain in 1492. Thereafter, in both French and British literature, the gypsies, as they became known, became transfigured by the literary imagination into a collective trope (conjoining freedom and escape from the everyday, licentiousness, thievery, exoticness, foreignness, and the ability to read the future) and a narrative device (the child stolen by gypsies or the adult who runs away with them, as in Arnold's "The Scholar-Gypsy" [1853] or Borrow's *The Romany Rye* of the same year). Gypsies by the nineteenth century were firmly established archetypes of the romantic imagination and the Gothic tale as much as they were actual people roaming the byways of the English and French countryside. As David Mayall notes,

From *Papers on Language and Literature* 44, no. 3 (Summer 2008): 305–27. © 2008 by the Board of Trustees, Southern Illinois University at Edwardsville.

> the Gypsies have [...] held especial appeal for the bohemian
> imagination of artists, poets, dramatists and fiction writers [...].
> In fine art and "high-brow" literature, in the less "respectable"
> penny dreadfuls and railway literature, and in both light and
> serious operas, the Gypsies regularly appear in the familiar guise
> of exotic, dark-skinned, nomadic and romantically alluring rural
> nomads. (139)

As we know, *Jane Eyre* has a famous gypsy interlude when Rochester assumes the guise of a gypsy fortuneteller to interrogate Jane, and in *The Mill on the Floss*, Maggie as a little girl runs away briefly to join the gypsies.[1]

Throughout the nineteenth century, novelists and poets drew on gypsies to represent a complex of meanings. Balzac, for instance, makes brief mention of them as figures of escape, exotica, and fortune-telling in eleven of his novels, Louisa May Alcott in eight novels deploys the gypsies as a trope for outdoor pleasure and sexual licentiousness, and Edward Bulwer-Lytton in countless volumes invokes the gypsies as the dark ancestors of possibly dangerous characters. To characterize someone as a gypsy in the nineteenth-century novel is to bring in a host of negative connotations ranging from criminality to miscegenation. Estella's terrifying convict mother has gypsy blood in *Great Expectations*, Heathcliff's mysterious darkness and dangerousness stem from possible gypsy blood in *Wuthering Heights*, and Will Ladislaw's bohemian recklessness is explained by the inhabitants of Middlemarch as a product of gypsy parentage.

Real gypsies were shunned during this period for allied reasons. As Celia Espuglas has set out, these reasons were underlaid by racism; eighteenth- and nineteenth-century European accounts stressed the absolute racial apartness of gypsies as well as their status as a "degenerate" breed of humankind.[2] Gypsies were also disliked because they refused to fit into the prevailing economic system, relying instead on "fortune-telling, hawking secondhand goods, and clearing discarded waste" to make money (Espuglas 148). Grellmann's 1783 account of the gypsies, for instance, focused on the gypsies as indolent; Leo Lucassen notes that even when they worked as, for instance, musicians or hawkers, such activities were often a form of indirect intimidation and thievery (75).[3] Moreover, their standards of hygiene and cleanliness were far less stringent than those held by the typical British citizen—gypsies often left bodily waste in open trenches near their encampments and were renowned for their dirtiness and aversion to baths. Gypsies also had a reputation, probably merited to some degree, for unrestrained licentiousness and prostitution; certainly the figure of the female gypsy as an enticing alien (her descent from Cleopatra was legendary[4]) marked depictions such as that by George Crabbe:

in his "The Lovers' Journey" Crabbe described a gypsy woman whose "light laugh and roguish leer express'd / The vice implanted in her youthful breast" (158–59). When one adds to this the popular idea that gypsies stole children (Espuglas 148), it is not too difficult to see why "respectable" citizens feared and avoided them. While rare, there are accounts of gypsies during the eighteenth and nineteenth centuries actually stealing children on occasion, sometimes to keep them, sometimes for the purpose of ransom. For instance, one three-year-old child snatched in 1727 was Adam Smith, who later authored *Wealth of Nations*; he was snatched back, however, by a search party a few hours later (Ross 18).

Before and during the nineteenth century, fictional literature made wide use of these child snatchings, employing the narrative device of the child stolen by gypsies to a degree grossly out of proportion to historical reality. The tale of little Adam Smith became a springboard for a raft of nursery tales, all carrying a heavyweight of admonition, as Deborah Epstein Nord has pointed out: "If the great Smith, a man so important to the building of British civilization, found himself in danger of absorption into an alien tribe, so, too, might any careless child" (*Gypsies* 24). But child kidnapping and the later restoration of the lost child as an adult also appeared in nineteenth-century texts meant for an adult audience, such as Scott's *Guy Mannering* (1815), Men Pickering's *Nan Darrell, or the gypsy mother* (1831), Hugo's *The Hunchback of Notre Dame* (1831), Mérimée's *Carmen* (1845), and Wilkie Collins's *Armadale* (1866), among many, many others.[5] This plot device was appealing partly because of its sensationalism, but also because the child stolen by gypsies reformulates an ancient device of romance where a child is sold to or stolen by a group of outsiders. This motif we recognize at least as far back as in the selling of Joseph by his brothers to the Ishmaelites in Genesis and later in the fifth or sixth century A.D. Roman tale that gave Shakespeare the plot for *Pericles*, in which pirates steal the hero's daughter. In each tale, there is a later reunion with the family after much hardship.

Gypsies are not a usual feature of Austen's world, nor in general does she use so directly the figures and plot devices of romance. In *Emma*, however, there the gypsies are, front and center. In the famous gypsy episode in *Emma*, Harriet Smith, Emma's protégée, falls briefly into the hands of gypsies, who harass her and try to steal her purse until she is rescued by Frank Churchill, a handsome young man who happens on the scene. Most critics explain the gypsy subplot in terms of the thematic opposition the novel asserts between social realism and romance, for the night before the gypsy interlude, Harriet had been at a ball in which she was shunned publicly by Mr. and Mrs. Elton. Mr. Knightley, the novel's hero, had come to the rescue and escorted Harriet into the dance. Emma's later confusion about which rescue Harriet had valued,

Mr. Knightley's at the dance or Frank Churchill's with the gypsies, helps complicate the love plot; the undoing of the confusion makes Austen's moral and social point that Mr. Knightley's rescue was far more valuable to Harriet (and presumably to right-thinking readers) than was Frank Churchill's.[6] As Nord argues, "Austen seems to be commenting on the insularity of Emma's world, a world in which stories of danger and romance result from the mildest contact with figures whose meanings themselves derive from stories and myth" ("'Marks of Race'" 194).

This line of interpretation is true enough. But the gypsies nonetheless seem odd figures; their presence complicates other issues in the novel with concision and irony. Austen plays with the conventions of gypsies for her own purposes—partly to mock romantic conventions, partly to create complex resonances between these conventions and her own plot and characters. Austen employs in particular two constituent elements of the romantic archetype of the gypsy—the purported ability to tell the future and the purported desire to steal children. Both create ironic reverberations with Emma's own future-telling (matchmaking) and her desire to create a family romance for Harriet Smith, giving her a noble or at least gentrified lineage. The gypsies' historical identity as putative invaders, outsiders who are understood as having no respect for English laws or class structure, is also important, for Austen participates in the view that gypsies, as non-racially English, must be understood as operating beyond all usual cultural constraints.[7] Thus Harriet's illegitimacy and her role as a relative outsider in Highbury society (she is only a parlor boarder at a local school) mean that Harriet herself has some uneasy consonances with the gypsies who attack her. In particular, the gypsies' putative sexual license underwrites a chief anxiety about what might happen to a beautiful young lady taken unawares in the road, which happens to Harriet. Moreover, the gypsies' freedom of movement as well as their freedom in regards to property and sexuality—augmented by their capacity for social subversion—stands in a variety of specific structural contrasts to the social orthodoxies of Emma's world. Last, the gypsies can operate as a species of *deus ex machines*. They do not resolve the plot, it is true, but they provide a new red herring that generates plot complications in ways that ultimately make possible the novel's comic ending.

Austen would have known about gypsies through literature, through evangelical writings, and through experience. Literary representations of the gypsies abounded in the late eighteenth and early nineteenth centuries. Gypsies had become something of a literary fad in the two decades following the 1787 English translation of Heinrich Grellmann's 1784 treatise on gypsies (Mayall 152). At least three texts we *know* Austen read cite the gypsies, and there were surely countless others. Richardson, Austen's favorite author, mentions them in *Clarissa* (Lovelace says, "'I know not who could escape the sweet gypsies, whose fascinating powers are so much aided by our own raised imaginations'" (5: 207), while Matthew Lewis's 1796 *The Monk*, referenced in *Northanger Abbey* by the vile John Thorpe (48), begins with a gypsy woman's prediction of the eventual death of the heroine.[8] Austen also knew and loved Goldsmith's 1766 *The Vicar of Wakefield*, in which yet another gypsy prophecy begins a long series of woes for the protagonist and his family. She was very likely also aware of Wordsworth's 1807 "Gypsies," in which the gypsies' sedentary habits in their camp are contrasted to the world of progressive imagination and labor the poet inhabits, as well as to the world of vagrancy and continual movement Wordsworth understands as the gypsies' more proper sphere.[9]

Austen's interest in evangelicalism and evangelicals probably also led her to the many tracts and magazine articles of the early nineteenth century that proposed reforms for the gypsies.[10] As Mayall notes, "much of the published writing on Gypsies [...] thus grew out of the contemporary [...] evangelical zeal to first understand and then reform this group of itinerants who flaunted their heathenism on the domestic shores" (154). In general, evangelicals saw the gypsies as a "race desperately in need of being rescued from their wayward, amoral and irreligious lives and being assimilated into respectable and settled society" (155). It is true that Austen's treatment of the gypsies in *Emma* shows no reformist impulse at all, but Austen was probably aware of the many articles in such journals as the *Church of England Magazine*, the *Christian Observer*, or the *Christian Herald* that promoted such reform (Mayall 155–56).

Last, Austen probably knew gypsies from experience as well as from her reading. Gypsies were a common sight in the English countryside, sometimes at nomadic encampments such as that depicted in *Emma*—and sometimes at more long-term encampments such as that at Wandsworth, the Potteries, and Kirk Yetholm in mid- and northern England (Mayall 157) and Surrey, Southhampton, and Farnham in the south (Kramp 164n). We know that Austen was a stickler for a certain kind of geographical realism, refusing, for instance, to use hedgerows in *Mansfield Park* once she learned that they were not common in Northhamptonshire where the novel is set, so it is very unlikely that she would have placed gypsies in her novel if they were an improbable addition.[11] After all, Austen's contemporaries, Wordsworth and Clare, write multiple poems implying that when one is out for a rural walk, one is as likely as not to pass a gypsy encampment. Confirmation that Austen probably herself saw gypsies in her youth comes from the fact that Hampshire, the home of her childhood, is known in Romany as *baulo mengresky tem*, or "sheepherder's country," according to George Borrow, the main populizer of gypsydom in the nineteenth century; the gypsies named the places they themselves roamed, and thus they likely roamed Hampshire as often as they did other English counties.[12] Certainly, Austen's treatment of the gypsies in *Emma* seems to imply that everyone in Emma's world, and, presumably, everyone in the world of Austen's original readership, knows all they need to know about gypsies, that they are an entirely known quantity even though they are outsiders. They are the familiar exotic.

Perhaps this presumption of familiarity explains why the gypsies come onto the scene in *Emma* in a way opposed to the romance tradition in almost every particular. First, Austen gives us none of the usual colorful details about the gypsies' costumes, tents, or paraphernalia, no description of their physical presence with an eye to elevating their mystery or romance. There is no mention of the gaudily painted wagons that were a staple of gypsy culture, nor the vivid shawls and bangles so often referenced in contemporary works such as the "red cloak and . . . broad-brimmed gypsy hat tied down with a striped handkerchief" Rochester wears to impersonate a gypsy fortuneteller in *Jane Eyre* (Brontë 197). All that connects them to the traditional gypsy camp of romance is that they are found along a secluded part of the road under the deep shade of branched elms, along what Austen calls a "broader patch of greensward" (*Emma* 333)—"greensward," incidentally, being an archaic term Austen uses nowhere else in her fiction.

Second, the gypsies who trouble Harriet are not a crew of men and women, but rather "half a dozen children, headed by a stout woman and a great boy" (333). The composition of the gypsy crew undermines for the reader the most basic and conventional fear that would otherwise accompany an attack on a young woman: that of sexual attack. These gypsies want more than the shilling Harriet offers them, but they would be content with her whole purse. Further, when Frank Churchill comes along to chase the gypsies away, he comes on foot rather than on horseback; on foot he makes far less a figure of chivalric rescue than he would were he mounted. Austen is careful to give a reason for Frank's being without his horse: "The pleasantness of the morning had induced him to walk forward, and leave his horses to meet him by another road, a mile or two beyond Highbury" (334). In fact, as we can deduce later, he is on foot because he wanted one last chance to see Jane Fairfax before his departure from the town, and walking to return some scissors to Mrs. and Miss Sates provided him with an adequate excuse. But while here Austen is developing her mystery romance between Frank and Jane, she is also demythologizing the gypsy encounter. Frank confronts the gypsies; how we do not learn, but the indirect discourse used to describe his relation of what happened seems to imply a certain level of brutality that Frank seems to admit without embarrassment: "The terror which the woman and boy had been creating in Harriet was then their own portion. He had left them completely frightened" (334). Frank's behavior toward a woman and several children seems, in fact, the reverse of chivalry. Further, Frank does not confront the adult male members of the gypsies who must be in the neighborhood; significantly, they are hidden away, neither visible nor effective. In a reverse of heroic behavior, Frank instead leaves Emma to alert Mr. Knightley, the magistrate, about "there being such a set of people in the neighborhood," and goes on his way (334).[13] The gypsies here at any rate pose no heroic threat and draw no heroic response, and their episode smacks far more of the comic-burlesque than it does of the heroic romance.

The romance traditions associated with gypsies are instead brought into play through irony. Emma's disastrous propensity for matchmaking, for instance, is set against gypsies' status as fortune-tellers. From the early pages of the novel, Emma and Mr. Knightley have sparred about whether her matchmaking for the newly-wedded Westons has just been "a lucky guess" (13) or success in a worthy endeavor. For his part, Mr. Woodhouse is sure that Emma's predictions are as good as any gypsy's; he complains, "'Ah! My dear, I wish you would not make matches and foretell things, for whatever you say always comes to pass'" (12). Later, when Emma first conceives of her match between Mr. Elton and Harriet, she muses, "It would be an excellent match; and only too palpably desirable, natural, and probable, for her to have much merit in planning it. She feared it was what every body else must think of and predict" (34–35). Matchmaking as prediction becomes conjoined with the gypsies once Emma begins to assume that Frank and Harriet are meant for each other. As Emma notes, "she could not but hope that the gypsy, though she had *told* no fortune, might be proved to have made Harriet's" (340; author's italics). What matters, thus, is how Emma fills in (ironically) for what one would expect the gypsies to do; she foretells in their stead.[14]

A similar reversal takes place regarding the gypsy motif of stealing children. Curiously, the gypsies attack Harriet during a time in which there are two relatively defenseless children about Highbury: Emma's nephews, Henry and John. Their parents, the John Knightleys, have left them with their grandfather and aunt, that is, Mr. Woodhouse and Emma, for several weeks. Given how protective their mother has been depicted earlier in the novel, it seems rather unrealistic that the boys would be allowed a visit without their parents, for Mr. Woodhouse is a loving but inattentive guardian, and Emma is much involved with her own schemes and socializing. But Austen is willing to indulge in a relatively improbable circumstance to place the boys there, parentless, just at the time of the gypsy incident, just *perceptibly* to remind the reader of the threat gypsies pose in romances: stealing children. Importantly, these children include the heir to Mr. Knightley's estate at Donwell Abbey:

the elder boy, Henry. That Henry is the heir has already been brought to the reader's attention when Emma earlier worried about his possible disinheritance were Mr. Knightley to marry Jane Fairfax; much later in the novel, she will blush to recall this concern when she herself is to marry Mr. Knightley and in so doing cut off her nephew's prospects. Thus Austen has subtly brought the romantic convention of an heir in peril, with gypsies lurking, into the imaginative penumbra of her novel. And this reminder of gypsies stealing children is there in turn to bring to the fore the issue of Harriet's parentage and Emma's desire to create a family romance for her.

Harriet needs a family romance to measure up to Emma's hopes for her social elevation. As Freud sets out, a family romance is one's persistent irrational belief or fantasy that one has been brought up by the wrong family, that one has been stolen by lowlifes or switched in the cradle, and that one's real, unknown family is far superior to the parents one seems actually to have.[15] Harriet herself has no such fantasy; she has never tried to find out who her parents are. Emma, however, is sure that Harriet comes from elevated stock. Early on, she advises Harriet:

> "The misfortune of your birth ought to make you particularly careful of your associates. There can be no doubt of your being a gentleman's daughter, and you must support your claim to that position by every thing within you own power, or there would be plenty of people who would take pleasure in degrading you." (30)

Harriet is both like the gypsies and like a child stolen by them in that no one knows from where and whom she comes.[16] As Michael Kramp points out, both Harriet and the gypsies "are 'natural'; neither Harriet nor the Romani have a definitive origin or social position" (150). Like a changeling child, Harriet could be anyone, high or low. The emphasis on her "blood," her unknown origins, underwrites her uneasy social status. No less an authority than Mr. Knightley offers the "degrading" view of Harriet that Emma warns her against; to Emma, he angrily claims, "'She is the natural daughter of nobody knows whom, with probably no settled provision at all, and certainly no respectable relations'" (61). And Emma, her patroness, will ultimately come to use much more "degrading" language once she finds out that Harriet is a tradesman's daughter. Austen's free indirect discourse gives us Emma's reflections:

> Such was the blood of gentility which Emma had formerly been so ready to vouch for!—It was as likely to be as untainted, perhaps, as the blood of many a gentleman: but what a connexion had she

been preparing for Mr. Knightley—or for the Churchills—or even for Mr. Elton!—The stain of illegitimacy, unbleached by nobility or wealth, would have been a stain indeed. (482)

This language of "stain" and contamination strikes modern readers as reprehensible but would have been unexceptionable to most of Austen's original audience.[17] And Harriet's tainted and stain-making blood connects her to the gypsies, whose blood was putatively even more tainted; if not corralled into an approved marriage, Harriet could be hereafter, like the gypsies, an outsider to proper English society.[18]

Other elements of the gypsy episode reinforce Harriet's status as an outsider whose integration into Highbury is problematic. Harriet is not originally alone when she comes across the gypsies but is rather on a walk with one Miss Bickerton, another parlor boarder at Harriet's school. Miss Bickerton is so "excessively frightened" by the one gypsy child whom they first meet that she "[gives] a great scream, [. . .] [runs] up a steep bank, [clears] a slight hedge at the top, and [makes] the best of her way by a short cut back to Highbury" (333). Evidently, Miss Bickerton's status is even lower than Harriet's, as implied by her name ("Bickerton" seems to denote a town where people argue over trivia) and by her athletic and unladylike response to the gypsies, as she abandons Harriet in a great scramble. Why can't Harriet escape in the same way? Again, Austen's free indirect discourse offers what must have been the substance of Harriet's explanation: "She had suffered very much from cramp after dancing, and her first attempt to mount the bank brought on such a return of it as made her absolutely powerless—and in this state, and exceedingly terrified, she had been obliged to remain" (333).[19] Harriet's cramp thus links the gypsy episode back to the Crown ball and Mr. Knightley's rescue. In the chapter before, the reader had last seen Harriet exuberantly dancing, joyful and grateful to escape the snubs of the Eltons, "the cruel state of things before" giving way to "very complete enjoyment and very high sense of the distinction which her happy features announced." We are told "she bounded higher than ever, flew farther down the middle, and was in a continual course of smiles" (328). All this bounding and flying led to cramp, and both the bounding and flying as well as the cramp suggests that Harriet perhaps does not completely belong in Highbury society, that she is both too physically rambunctious *and* too physically inapt. Her physical paralysis in the face of her returned cramp from dancing calls forth atavistic fears of rape, for she is lying on the ground as the gypsies approach. This intimation of rape (the reader does not at this point know the sex and age of the gypsies who assail her, though this information is provided shortly and will make plain that she is in no sexual danger) reminds the reader of yet another way Harriet could be rendered socially untouchable, almost as untouchable as the gypsies whom she encounters.

The gypsies' arrival on the scene also plays a key ironic role in developing the plot, to "reinvigorate a storyline" that seems on "the verge of resolution," as Elizabeth Lorang argues (1). Gypsies are themselves traditionally known as story-tellers, of course, and in *Emma* one of their roles is to get a story reawakened at a point of relative narrative quiescence. The gypsies enter the plot in the third chapter of the third volume. The second volume of *Emma* has concluded with the news that Frank Churchill is to return to Highbury, and Emma's reflections on those tidings begin volume three, reflections that make plain that the Emma/Frank romantic plot has lost its steam, probably irrevocably: "Her own attachment had subsided into a mere nothing" (315). While Emma still believes wrongly that Frank has romantic feelings for her, she also believes that those feelings are subsiding as well: "It was a clear thing he was less in love than he had been," she muses (316). The Harriet/Mr. Elton plot has also come to a dead end, for, as we know, the chapter before the gypsies' interruption treats the ball during which Mr. Elton displays his cruelty to Harriet and Harriet learns in consequence that the idealized Mr. Elton of her imagination never existed: "It seemed as if her eyes were suddenly opened, and she were enabled to see that Mr. Elton was not the superior creature she had believed him" (332). The very chapter that will contain the gypsies begins with a summation of how things stand from Emma's point of view: "Harriet rational, Frank Churchill not too much in love, and Mr. Knightley not wanting to quarrel with her, how very happy a summer must be before her!" (332). There is much wrong with Emma's idea of great happiness, particularly her preference for a continued fruitless and low-key courtship from Frank and her reduction of Mr. Knightley's role to that of "not quarreling with her," but her depiction of the status quo reveals the plot's stasis at this point. Emma's satisfaction with stasis is itself one major flaw among others that Austen's plot will work to correct.

The gypsies start the plot up again by presenting Emma with a new red herring to pursue and a new matchmaking venture: Harriet and Frank, who she assumes will be drawn together, as all romance heroines and heroes are, through the hero's daring rescue of the heroine. Chastened by the Elton debacle, Emma resolves not to speak of her hopes to Harriet or anyone else. But privately her hopes are given wide play, and she, not the gypsies, tells a fortune for Harriet. After all, the lockstep logic of rescues transfigured into romance seems so obvious to Emma that she is sure that even were she to present the case to male analytic intelligences, they would concur with her: "Could a linguist, could a grammarian, could even a mathematician have seen what she did, have witnessed their appearance together, and heard their history of it, without feeling that circumstances had been at work to make them peculiarly interesting to each other?" (335). We know, of course, that she has employed similar logic when she earlier deduced that Mr. Dixon and Jane Fairfax have romantic feelings for each other; had not Mr. Dixon at Weymouth rescued Jane in a boating mishap from an almost certain fall overboard? As Lorang argues, "From the melodramatic intrusion of the gypsies, [...] the action of the last third of the book builds" (1): Emma's mistake about Harriet masks Harriet's interest in Mr. Knightley, while Emma's mistake about Frank masks Frank's interest in Jane Fairfax. When at the climax of the book Emma discovers who Harriet truly felt was her "rescuer," (i.e., Mr. Knightley rather than Frank—the former rescue Harriet terms "'a much more precious circumstance'" [406]) and that Emma may have lost Mr. Knightley to Harriet, we see the logical culmination of the gypsies' intervention. Because Emma has appropriated the gypsies' fortune-telling, her own fortune as one self-deceived has been set.

By the end of the chapter that introduces them, the gypsies have been reabsorbed into the repetitions of romance, for the gypsy adventure has been reduced to a story demanded by Emma's nephews: "Harry and John were still asking every day for the story of Harriet and the gypsies, and still tenaciously setting [Emma] right if she varied in the slightest particular from the original recital" (336). As children do, Harry and John demand exactitude in a story's repetition, but their doing so also shows how quickly and thoroughly Harriet's adventure has become lore, gypsy lore.[20] Interestingly, we do not know the details of the account the little boys were told. It no doubt varies from the tale as we have it in the narrative, where indirect discourse gives us a summary of what both Harriet and Frank had related, with the events before Frank's entrance presumably told by Harriet and those after presumably told by Frank. Whose voice says, however, of the gypsy assault, "How the trampers might have behaved, had the young ladies been more courageous, must be doubtful; but such an invitation for attack could not be resisted" (333) or "her terror and her purse were too tempting, and she was followed, or rather surrounded, by the whole gang, demanding more" (334)? This judgment on the appeal of weakness to the predatory belongs to either Emma or the narrator, or both, but at any rate stands as an instance of what Emma's nephews were *not* told, what was *not* repeated. "The story of Harriet and the gypsies" is thus a cautionary romance tale more in line with the nursery tales about little Adam Smith; the relation of what happens to Harriet and the gypsies in the novel itself is much more. The gypsies themselves disappear, long before Mr. Knightley as magistrate has been notified of their presence—they have performed their thematic and narrative duties and may as well be off. "The gipsies [sic] did not wait for the operations of justice; they took themselves off in a hurry" (336).

There are two last touches of the gypsies in the novel. One occurs in
Mrs. Elton's deliciously awful plans for the outing at Donwell Abbey. She has
a yearning to play Marie Antoinette (with a donkey rather than sheep) and to
dine *al fresco* (Folsom 160). As she dictates to Mr. Knightley,

> "There is to be no form or parade—a sort of gipsy party.—We are
> to walk about your gardens, and gather the strawberries ourselves,
> and sit under trees, and whatever else you may like to provide, it is
> to be all out of doors—a table spread in the shade, you know. Every
> thing as natural and simple as possible." (355)

Under the trees in the shade was, of course, where Harriet met the gypsies;
Austen thus hints at the dangers in Mrs. Elton's romantic pretensions. Mr.
Knightley goes on to explain that "'My idea of the simple and natural will be
to have the table spread in the dining-room. The nature and the simplicity
of gentlemen and ladies, with their servants and furniture, I think is best
observed by meals within doors'" (355). The indoors, gentility, servants,
furniture: with these touches, Mr. Knightley rebukes Mrs. Elton, the world
of the gypsies, and the romantic view of gypsies, all at the same time.

But Mr. Knightley has a reason ultimately to be grateful to the gypsies.
At the very end of the novel, it is unclear how Emma and Mr. Knightley
are to wed, given Mr. Woodhouse's objection to any change in his or his
daughter's life. But poultry-thieves come into the neighborhood, and Mr.
Woodhouse with his fear of "housebreakers" is glad to have a strong son-in-
law in the house; thus Mr. Knightley and Emma can marry. Austen does not
identify the poultry-thieves directly with the gypsies, though she calls the
turkey thefts "pilfering" conducted "by the ingenuity of man" (483).[21] I have
always preferred to believe, however, that the gypsies came back for a spell
to Highbury, to make the happy ending possible, just as fairies return at the
end of Act V in *A Midsummer Night's Dream* (a play the novel references at
another point) to give their blessing to the multiple nuptial beds of Theseus's
household.[22] The gypsies have done so much for the plot already that their
presence here as the last instigators of a comic ending seems appropriate.

In teaching *Emma*, I have often found that students initially judge the
gypsy episode as an improbable and clumsy exercise of narrative intervention.
Ultimately, it becomes apparent that the gypsies' intervention in *Emma* is
much more than a device by which the world of the romance intrudes upon
Highbury, but rather a concise critique and refiguring of the romantic tradition of the gypsy narrative as a whole. Though they inhabit the shady verges
of the novel, by implication the gypsies tell us much about the central characters, themes, and issues of the novel, underscoring the dangers inherent in

marginality and in romantic imagination. Their presence and their warnings linger even after they have roamed on.

NOTES

1. We most remember Eliot's gypsies from this episode in *The Mill in the Floss*, but gypsies were also the subject of one of her most popular poems in her lifetime, now rarely read, "The Spanish Gypsy" (1868).

2. Accounts from Grellmann, Hoyland, Borrow, and others all stressed the gypsy's racial apartness, including the strong gypsy disinclination for marriage outside the clan. One member of a clan of "very well known Gypsies in Shropshire" explains that "the most dreaded thing of all Romany parents is that a son or daughter may *prastra y frew romeo du gorgio*—run away and marry a house dweller" (Locke 19). Darwin assumed that gypsies never intermarry when he argued in his *The Descent of Man* (1871) that the gypsies stand as evidence to refute the idea that skin color follows from climate:

> Of all the differences between the races of man, the colour of the skin is the most conspicuous and one of the best marked. Differences of this kind, it was formerly thought, could be accounted for by long exposure under different climates [. . .]. The view has been rejected chiefly because the distribution of the variously coloured races, most of whom must have long inhabited their present homes, does not coincide with corresponding differences of climate. [. . .] The uniform appearance in various parts of the world of gypsies and Jews, though the uniformity of the latter has been somewhat exaggerated, is likewise an argument on the same side. (242)

Note that Darwin believed gypsies were a better case for uniformity of skin color despite pan-global dispersion than were Jews, who were equally if not more diasporic; thus Darwin implicitly argues that gypsies were more racially homogenous.

3. John Locke (no relation to the philosopher) wrote of his experiences in the 1920s as a gypsy child in Shropshire; while his account tells of gypsy life about one hundred and twenty years after Jane Austen's early adulthood, he also claims, as many gypsies do, that gypsy life remained relatively unchanged for centuries. One of ten children, Locke lists as gypsy occupations such endeavors as basketmaking (the baskets were then hawked) and horse-trading (he admits they would often "play a few tricks with horses when selling them to farmers and dealers" [16]), as well as fraud, poaching, and petty thievery in farmers' fields. See also Paul Nixon, who in canvassing the early twentieth-century writings incorporated in the *Journal of the Gypsy Lore Society*, notes the following occupations and services gypsies performed: "tinsmiths, blacksmiths, horse-traders, repairers, journeymen, traders, horticulturalists, occasional domestic servants, charmers, healers, counselors, and so forth" (457).

4. See Drew on Cleopatra as the gypsies' "grand-matra" (grandmother) (126).

5. Child kidnappings by gypsies were also common in the eighteenth-century British novel; for instance, Defoe's Moll Flanders is stolen by gypsies as a baby, as is Fielding's Joseph Andrews.

6. Deborah Epstein Nord summarizes this usual view of the thematic point of the gypsy episode: "Emma turns this incident into a tale of romance and chivalry, feeling sure that the potential lovers were thrown together by an unprecedented ordeal. Emma's misreading of the event is consistent with her misperceptions of romantic attachments throughout the novel" (*Gypsies* 15).

7. In her wide-ranging survey of literary representations of gypsies read against the historical record of the Holocaust, Katie Trumpener argues that gypsies constitute a specific challenge to Western Enlightenment values and that they are represented consistently as standing entirely apart from the Western cultures they move among:

> Moving through civil society, the Gypsies apparently remain beyond reach of everything that constitutes Western identity [. . .] outside of historical record and historical time, outside of Western law, the Western nation state, and Western economic orders, outside of writing and discursivity itself. [. . .] Despite their self-containment, paradoxically, the Gypsies' wildness is highly contagious, as their arrival in a new place initiates [. . .] a crisis for Enlightenment definitions of civilization and nationalistic definitions of culture. (860)

8. John Thorpe reveals a great deal about his reading habits when he claims, "there has not been a tolerably decent [novel] come out since Tom Jones, except the Monk" (48). We know Austen did not approve of either novel.

9. The sedentary gypsies attacked by Wordsworth brought forth a defense from Coleridge, as noted by James Garrett:

> the poet, without seeming to reflect that the poor tawny wanderers might probably have been tramping for weeks together through road and lane, over moor and mountain, and consequently must have been right glad to rest themselves, their children and cattle, for one whole day; and overlooking the obvious truth, that such repose might be quite necessary for *them*, as a walk of the same continuance was pleasing and healthful for the more fortunate poet. (Coleridge 7:137)

Garrett adjudges Wordsworth's poem not much more generously: "Based on the poem, the poet's encounter with the gypsies was anything but fortuitous for the reputation of either gypsies or Wordsworth" (605). See also Espuglas, 150, for a further discussion of the poem. Anne Janowitz has argued that Wordsworth and Clare depict the gypsy as a figure who, "managing to live off the commons and waste in an age of enclosure, returns as a quasi-fantastical double to the English cottager" (167). Janowitz notes also that a "large number of late-eighteenth and early nineteenth century poetic presentations of Gypsies do not prettify their lives, nor do they run predominantly on racialist categories" (167).

10. In 1814, Austen wrote to her niece, Fanny Knight, that "I am by no means convinced that we ought not all to be Evangelicals & am at least persuaded that they who are so from Reason and Feeling, must be happiest & safest" (*Selected Letters* 174). Taken with an earlier letter from the same year to Martha Lloyd in which she professes that England is a "Religious Nation, a Nation in spite of much Evil improving in Religion" (168), we can see her interest in evangelical reform. As a

staunch Anglican, Austen would have been interested in Anglican Evangelicanism (perhaps most famously represented by William Wilberforce), not the Evangelical movements of Methodists, Calvinists, Baptists and so on.

11. Austen's letter to her sister Cassandra of January 29, 1813, came as she was planning the composition of *Mansfield Park* "If you could discover whether Northhamptonshire is a country of hedgerows I should be glad again" (*Selected Letters* 132). Evidently Cassandra replied that there were no hedgerows; at any rate, Austen saved the hedgerows for *Persuasion*, set in Somersetshire, where hedgerows are numerous.

12. John Locke (note 3 above) details his family's roaming: they went to Shropshire, Shrewsbury, Herefordshire, Pembrokeshire, even into Yorkshire for the Doncaster Races, and then even more far afield on occasion to North Wales and Ireland.

13. The phrase "set of people in the neighborhood" cannot help but be contrasted with Austen's earlier marked use of the idea of social "sets," for the third chapter contrasts the "chosen and the best" (Mr. Knightley, the Westons, and Mr. Elton) with "a second set," of whom the most "come-at-able" are Mrs. and Miss Bates and Mrs. Goddard (20). Frank's remark is thus an understatement of significant ironic import, though there is no reason to believe that Frank would be aware of the irony.

14. John Clare, who with Wordsworth is responsible for the greatest number of Romantic poems which take gypsies as their subject, noted in his chapbook in 1794 that the gypsies were not really any good at prognostication. Instead, he pointed out that fortune-telling relied "nothing more [on] witchcraft than the knowledge of village gossips & the petty deceptions played off on believing ignorance" (*Prose* 35). Clare's description offers a startling consonance with the operations of Emma's fortune-telling, for hers is a "believing ignorance" that creates its own "petty deceptions"—the fortune-teller deceives herself.

15. Nord's treatment of the gypsy episode in *Emma* also focuses on the importance of the family romance to romantic tales of the gypsy, asking in particular how family romances for young women might work in narratives, given Freud's assumption that oedipal energies drive the formation of the family romance in young men ("'Marks of Race'" 189–92). She further focuses on the three-way rivalry implicit in the text among Emma, Jane Fairfax, and Harriet, aligning it with other racial narratives of dark- and light-haired women in competition (as in Scott's gypsy narrative of *Guy Mannering*), overlaid as such narratives are by issues of "authentic" heritage (she notes that Harriet and Jane both have problematic parentage, in that Jane's parents are dead and can do nothing for her ["'Marks of Race'" 194]).

16. It is of some interest that Austen implies that Harriet, like the gypsies, has no fixed abode. Though she lives with Mrs. Goddard, she will not be living there forever, as her schooling is already complete. Further, once she becomes Emma's intimate, we are told that she "for some weeks past [. . .] had been spending more than half her time [at Hartfield], and gradually getting to have a bed-room appropriated to herself" (57).

17. As Devoney Looser has argued, given the "dismal" situation of illegitimate children in Austen's day, Austen's point of view "might even be said to liberalize the discourse on illegitimacy in her time," for Harriet is given a happy ending with a farmer, Robert Martin. Since an illegitimate child was "not only legally an outcast, [. . .] but also morally tainted," this happy end implies that

Harriet's entry into the yeoman caste has banished whatever "taint" she might originally have carried (106).

18. Michael Kramp has pursued in detail the argument about Harriet's consonance with the gypsies along nationalistic and racial lines, focusing on Harriet's "whiteness" as the quality that makes it possible to turn her from an outsider like the gypsies into a symbol of England's desired future:

> Austen's use of the alien dark-skinned gypsies in juxtaposition to the native White woman allows the novelist to accentuate the Englishness of the latter by stressing the foreignness of the former. As an illegitimate and orphaned member of the "large and populous" village of Highbury, Harriet initially appears similar to the nomadic outsiders, but as a young, White, and anonymous female resident of this neighborhood, she also represents the future promise of her local and national community. (148)

I agree with Kramp that the novel evidences clear signs of English nationalism and xenophobia (see also Claudia Johnson on this subject, particularly 155–56), but tend to see the racial and national element as less central—partly because Austen says nothing about the gypsies' skin color, when she very well could. On the relation between fictional representations of gypsies and nationalism, particularly in regard to tensions between depictions of gypsies and the realist tradition, see Yahav-Brown's "Gypsies, Nomadism, and the Limits of Realism" (*MLN* 121.5 [2006]: 1124–47).

19. Harriet's attempt to "mount the bank" brings yet another consonance between her and the gypsies—"mountebank" in Austen's day meant a quack or shyster as well as an entertainer who fooled the public; Coleridge in *Biographia Literaria*, for instance, yokes "mountebank" with one who "picks your pocket" (*Major Works* 420).

20. Trumpener's treatment of the gypsy incident in *Emma* also focuses on the absorption into the annals of oral memory but views that movement into repetition much more darkly than do I: "In the wake of the Gypsies' disruptive passage, special care must be taken to hold on to a history that exists only as an oral tradition; the psychic trauma of social violence is subsumed into a narratological compulsion to repeat" (868). I would argue instead that the characters who have this "compulsion to repeat" are two small boys, whose pleasure in the narrative no doubt flows from the gypsies' exotic and dangerous allure; we are invited to assume that the boys would have been as interested in repeating the tale if Harriet had been attacked by pirates or any other figures from romantic tales.

21. Clare's "The Gypsy Camp" proffers support for this conjecture; not only are the gypsies described as a "quiet, pilfering, unprotected race," but they also are described in particular as contriving "midnight theft to hatch" (29). Roughly a half-century earlier, Henry Fielding also assumed that the gypsy pilfering ran to poultry and other livestock as such, for in *Tom Jones* when our hero feasts in a barn with the Gypsy King, the board is spread with "good Store of Bacon, Fowls, and Mutton" (512).

22. Emma cites "the course of true love never did run smooth" from *A Midsummer Night's Dream* (1.1.134) and then notes that "'A Hartfield edition of Shakespeare would have a long note on that passage'" (75). The multiple ways in which gypsy figuration became retold through the trope of the fairy in the nineteenth century is a complex one, but both fairies and gypsies represented the romantic outsider with

magic capacities (the gypsies' magic was their fortunetelling and "second sight"). Certainly, the dominant expression of the narrative of the stolen child shifts in the nineteenth century from a story about gypsies to a story about fairies (cf. Yeats's "The Stolen Child").

Works Cited

Austen, Jane. Emma. *The Novels of Jane Austen*. Ed. R. W. Chapman. 3rd ed. Vol. 3. Oxford: Oxford UP, 1933.

———. *Jane Austen: Selected Letters*. Ed. R. W. Chapman. Oxford: Oxford UP, 1985.

———. *Northanger Abbey. The Novels of Jane Austen*. Ed. R. W. Chapman. 3rd ed. Vol. 5. Oxford UP, 1934.

Borrow, George. "Romane Navior of Temes and Gavior: Gypsy Names of Countries and Towns." *Romano Lavo-Lil. Word-Book of the Romany or, English Gypsy Language with Specimens of Gypsy Poetry, and an Accont [sic] of Certain Gysyries or Places Inhabited by Them, and of Varios [sic] Things Relating to Gypsy Life in England*. [1874.] Project Gutenberg. http://snowy.arsc.alaska.edu/mirrors/gutenberg/etext01/rmlav10h.html. Accessed Jan. 06, 2007.

Brontë, Charlotte. *Jane Eyre*. Ed. Beth Newman. *Case Studies in Contemporary Criticism*. Series ed. Ross C. Murfin. Boston: Bedford/St. Martin's: 1996.

Clare, John. "The Gypsy Camp." *The Later Poems of John Clare, 1837–1864*. Ed. Eric Robinson and David Powell. Vol. 1. Oxford: Clarendon Press, 1995. 29.

———. *The Prose of John Clare*. Ed. J.W. Tibble and Anne Tibble. London: Routledge, 1951.

Coleridge, Samuel Taylor. *Biographia Literaria: The Collected Works of Samuel Taylor Coleridge*. Ed. James Engell and W. Jackson Bate. Vol. 7. Princeton: Princeton UP, 1983.

———. *Samuel Taylor Coleridge: The Major Works*. Ed. H. J. Jackson. Oxford: Oxford UP, 1985.

Crabbe, George. "The Lover's Journey." *The Poetical Works of the Rev. George Crabbe*. Vol. 5. London: John Murray, 1834. 21–35.

Darwin, Charles. *The Descent of Man*. Vol. 1. London: John Murray, 1871.

Drew, John. "Gypsy Fortune-Telling in England." *British and American Studies* n.v. (1998): 125–31.

Espuglas, Celia. "Gypsy Women in English Life and Literature." *The Foreign Woman in British Literature: Exotics, Aliens, and Outsiders*. Ed. Marilyn Demarest Button and Toni Reed. Westport, CT: Greenwood Press, 1999. 145–58.

Fielding, Henry. *Tom Jones*. Ed. Sheridan Baker. New York: Norton, 1973.

Folsom, Marcia McClintock. "'I Wish We Had a Donkey': Small-Group Work and Writing Assignments for *Emma*." *Approaches to Teaching Austen's Emma*. Ed. Marcia McClintock Folsom. New York: Modern Language Association of America, 2004. 159–68.

Grellmann, Heinrich. [1784.] *Dissertation, on, the Gipsies, Being an, Historical Enquiry Concerning the Manner of Life, Economy, Customs and Conditions of these People in, Europe, and their Origin,*. Trans. Matthew Raper. London: n.p., 1787.

Hoyland, John. *A Historical Survey of the Customs, Habits, & Present State of the Gypsies; Designed to Develop the Origin of the Singular People, and to Promote the Amelioration of their Condition*. York: William Alexander, 1816.

Janowitz, Anne. "Clare Among the Gypsies." *Wordsworth Circle* 29.3 (1998) 167–71.

Johnson, Claudia. "'Not at All What a Man Should Be': Remaking English Manhood in *Emma*." *Critical Essays on Jane Austen*. Ed. Laura Mooneyham White. New York: G.K. Hall, 1998. 146–59.

Kramp, Michael. "The Woman, the Gypsies, and England: Harriet Smith's National Role." *College Literature* 31.1 (2004): 147–68.

Locke, John. "Gypsy Life in Shropshire—As It Was and As It Is." *Journal of the Gypsy Lore Society* 1 (1974): 14–21.

Looser, Devoney. "'A Very Kind Undertaking': *Emma* and Eighteenth-Century Feminism." *Approaches to Teaching Austen's Emma.* Ed. Marcia McClintock Folsom. New York: Modern Language Association of America, 2004. 100–109.

Lorang, Elizabeth. "Austen's Use of *Deus ex Machina* as a Complication of the Plot." Unpublished manuscript, 2006.

Lucassen, Leo. "Under the Cloak of Begging? Gypsy Occupations in Western Europe in the 19th and 20th Centuries." *Ethnologist Europaea* 23 (1993): 75–94.

Mayall, David. *Gypsy Identities, 1500–2000: From Egipcyans and Moon-men to the Ethnic Romany.* London: Routledge, 2004.

Nixon, Paul. "Life Patterns, Hazards, and Ascendancies: Gypsies, Tinkers and Travellers in Great Britain and Ireland." *Music, Language, and Literature of the Roma and Sinti.* Ed. Max Peter Baumann. Berlin: Verlag für Wissenschaft und Bildung, 2000. 453–460.

Nord, Deborah Epstein. *Gypsies and the British Imagination, 1807–1930.* New York: Columbia UP, 2006.

———. "'Marks of Race': Gypsy Figures and Eccentric Femininity in Nineteenth-Century Women's Writing." *Victorian Studies* 41.2 (1998): 189–210.

Richardson, Samuel. *Clarissa.* 8 vols. Dublin: P. Byrne, J. Moore, and A. Grueber, 1792.

Ross, Ian Simpson. *The Life of Adam Smith.* Oxford: Clarendon Press, 1995.

Trumpener, Katie. "The Time of the Gypsies: A 'People Without History' in the Narratives of the West." *Critical Inquiry* 18.4 (1992): 843–84.

Chronology

1775	Jane Austen is born on December 16 in the village of Steventon, Hampshire, to George Austen, parish clergyman, and Cassandra Leigh Austen. She is the seventh of eight children. She and her sister Cassandra are educated at Oxford and Southampton by the widow of a principal of Brasenose College, and then they attend the Abbey School at Reading. Jane's formal education ends when she is nine years old.
1787–1793	Austen writes various pieces for the amusement of her family (collected in the three volumes of *Juvenilia*), the most famous of which is *Love and Friendship*. She and her family also perform various plays and farces, some of which are written by Jane, in the family barn.
1793–1797	Austen writes her first novel, the epistolary *Lady Susan*, and begins the epistolary *Elinor and Marianne*, which will become *Sense and Sensibility*.
1796–1797	Austen completes *First Impressions*, an early version of *Pride and Prejudice*. Her father tries to get it published without success. Austen begins *Sense and Sensibility* and *Northanger Abbey*.
1798	Austen finishes a version of *Northanger Abbey*.
1801–1802	George Austen retires to Bath with his family. Jane probably suffers from an unhappy love affair (the man in question is believed to have died suddenly), and also probably becomes engaged for a day to Harris Bigg-Wither.

1803	Austen sells two-volume manuscript entitled *Susan* to a publisher for ten pounds. It is advertised but never printed. This is a version of *Northanger Abbey*, probably later revised.
1803–1805	Austen writes ten chapters of *The Watsons*.
1805–1806	George Austen dies. Jane abandons work on *The Watsons*. She, her mother, and her sister live in various lodgings in Bath.
1806–1809	The three Austen women move to Southampton, living near one of Jane's brothers.
1809	Jane, her sister, and her mother move to Chawton Cottage, in Hampshire, which is part of the estate of Jane's brother Edward Austen (later Knight), who has been adopted by Thomas Knight, a relative. Edward has just lost his wife, who died giving birth to her tenth child, and the household has been taken over by Jane's favorite niece, Fanny.
1811	Austen decides to publish *Sense and Sensibility* at her own expense and anonymously. It appears in November in a three-volume edition.
1811–1812	Austen is probably revising *First Impressions* extensively and beginning *Mansfield Park*.
1813	*Pride and Prejudice* is published in January. A second edition of it, as well as a second edition of *Sense and Sensibility*, come out in November.
1814	*Mansfield Park* is published anonymously. Austen begins *Emma*.
1815	Austen completes *Emma* and begins *Persuasion*. *Emma* is published anonymously by a new publisher.
1816	A second edition of *Mansfield Park* is published.
1817	A third edition of *Pride and Prejudice* is published. Austen begins *Sanditon*. She moves to Winchester, where she dies, after a yearlong illness, on July 18. She is buried in Winchester Cathedral.
1818	*Persuasion* and *Northanger Abbey* are published posthumously together, their authorship still officially anonymous.

Contributors

HAROLD BLOOM is Sterling Professor of the Humanities at Yale University. He is the author of 30 books, including *Shelley's Mythmaking*, *The Visionary Company*, *Blake's Apocalypse*, *Yeats*, *A Map of Misreading*, *Kabbalah and Criticism*, *Agon: Toward a Theory of Revisionism*, *The American Religion*, *The Western Canon*, and *Omens of Millennium: The Gnosis of Angels, Dreams, and Resurrection*. *The Anxiety of Influence* sets forth Professor Bloom's provocative theory of the literary relationships between the great writers and their predecessors. His most recent books include *Shakespeare: The Invention of the Human*, a 1998 National Book Award finalist, *How to Read and Why*, *Genius: A Mosaic of One Hundred Exemplary Creative Minds*, *Hamlet: Poem Unlimited*, *Where Shall Wisdom Be Found?*, and *Jesus and Yahweh: The Names Divine*. In 1999, Professor Bloom received the prestigious American Academy of Arts and Letters Gold Medal for Criticism. He has also received the International Prize of Catalonia, the Alfonso Reyes Prize of Mexico, and the Hans Christian Andersen Bicentennial Prize of Denmark.

MAAJA A. STEWART is professor emerita at the School of Liberal Arts of Tulane University. She is the author of *Domestic Realities and Imperial Fictions: Jane Austen's Novels in Eighteenth-Century Contexts*.

BARBARA Z. THADEN is an associate professor at St. Augustine's College in Raleigh, North Carolina. She is the author of *New Essays on the Maternal Voice in the Nineteenth Century* and the *Student Companion to Charlotte and Emily Bronte*.

SUSAN MORGAN is a professor at Miami University. She is the author of *Sisters in Time: Imagining Gender in Nineteenth-Century British Fiction*, *In the Meantime: Character and Perception in Jane Austen's Fiction*, and many other writings on Austen.

SARAH EMSLEY teaches in the Expository Writing Program at Harvard University. She has authored *Jane Austen's Philosophy of the Virtues* and is editor of *Jane Austen and the North Atlantic*.

ISOBEL GRUNDY is a professor emerita at the University of Alberta. She has published an extensive biography entitled *Lady Mary Wortley Montagu, Comet of the Enlightenment*, and is co-author/editor of *The Feminist Companion to Literature in English*. She was one of the producers of *Orlando: Women's Writing in the British Isles from the Beginnings to the Present*, which was published online.

JOHN WILTSHIRE is a professor at La Trobe University, Australia. His work includes *Jane Austen and the Body: "The Picture of Health"* and *Recreating Jane Austen*. Also, he is the editor of *Mansfield Park* in *The Cambridge Edition of the Works of Jane Austen*. He is a frequent speaker at Jane Austen Society meetings in North America and Australia.

IVOR MORRIS has been a university lecturer. He is the author of *Jane Austen and the Interplay of Character* and *Mr. Collins Considered: Approaches to Jane Austen*, among other works.

JULIET MCMASTER is professor emerita at the University of Alberta and founder of the Juvenilia Press. She is the author of *Jane Austen on Love* and *Jane Austen the Novelist* and co-editor of *The Cambridge Companion to Jane Austen*. She is a founding member of the Jane Austen Society of North America.

LAURA MOONEYHAM WHITE is an associate professor at the University of Nebraska–Lincoln. Her publications include *Romance, Language, and Education in Jane Austen's Novels* and *Critical Essays on Jane Austen*.

Bibliography

Berendsen, Marjet. *Reading Character in Jane Austen's* Emma. Assen, Netherlands: Van Gorcum, 1991.

Booth, Wayne C. "Point of View and the Control of Distance in *Emma*." *Nineteenth-Century Fiction* 16, no. 2 (September 1961): 95–116.

Byrne, Paula, ed. *Jane Austen's* Emma: *A Sourcebook*. London; New York: Routledge, 2004.

Dabundo, Laura, ed. *Jane Austen and Mary Shelley and Their Sisters*. Lanham, Md.: University Press of America, 2000.

———. "A Marriage of True Minds: The Community of Faith in Wordsworth and Austen." *Wordsworth Circle* 35, no. 2 (Spring 2004): 69–72.

Deresiewicz, William. *Jane Austen and the Romantic Poets*. New York: Columbia University Press, 2004.

DiPaolo, Marc. *Emma Adapted: Jane Austen's Heroine from Book to Film*. New York: Peter Lang, 2007.

Emsley, Sarah. *Jane Austen's Philosophy of the Virtues*. New York: Palgrave Macmillan, 2005.

Erkan, Ayça Ülker. "The Portrayal of the Interaction between the Individuals and Society in Jane Austen's *Emma*." *Interactions: Aegean Journal of English and American Studies/Ege Ingiliz ve Amerikan Incelemeleri Dergisi* 12 (2003): 9–20.

Folsom, Marcia McClintock, ed. *Approaches to Teaching Austen's* Emma. New York: Modern Language Association of America, 2004.

Galperin, William H. *The Historical Austen*. Philadelphia: University of Pennsylvania Press, 2003.

Gard, Roger. *Jane Austen's Novels: The Art of Clarity*. New Haven: Yale University Press, 1992.

Gill, Richard, and Susan Gregory. *Mastering the Novels of Jane Austen*. Houndmills, Basingstoke, Hampshire; New York: Palgrave Macmillan, 2003.

Gohrisch, Jana. "'Indifferent Differences': Everyday Life in Jane Austen's *Emma*." *Journal for the Study of British Cultures* 6, no. 2 (1999): 153–66.

Graham, Peter. *Jane Austen & Charles Darwin: Naturalists and Novelists*. Aldershot, England; Burlington, Vt.: Ashgate, 2008.

Gross, Gloria Sybil. *In a Fast Coach with a Pretty Woman: Jane Austen and Samuel Johnson*. New York: AMS, 2002.

———. "Mentoring Jane Austen: Reflections on 'My Dear Dr. Johnson.'" *Persuasions* 16, no. 11 (December 1989): 53–60.

Hagan, John; "The Closure of *Emma*." *SEL: Studies in English Literature, 1500–1900* 15, no. 4 (Autumn 1975): 545–61.

Hecimovich, Gregg A. *Austen's* Emma. London; New York: Continuum, 2008.

Hudson, Glenda. *Sibling Love and Incest in Jane Austen's Fiction*. New York: St. Martin's Press, 1992.

Johnson, Claudia L. *Jane Austen: Women, Politics, and the Novel*. Chicago: University of Chicago Press, 1988.

Jones, Darryl. *Jane Austen*. New York: Palgrave Macmillan, 2004.

Jones, Hazel. *Jane Austen and Marriage*. London; New York: Continuum, 2009.

Koppel, Gene. *The Religious Dimension of Jane Austen's Novels*. Ann Arbor, Mich.: UMI Research Press, 1988.

Kreisel, Deanna K. "Where Does the Pleasure Come From? The Marriage Plot and Its Discontents in Jane Austen's *Emma*." *Persuasions* 29 (2007): 217–226.

Kuwahara, Kuldip Kaur. "Jane Austen's *Emma* and Empire: A Postcolonial View." *Persuasions* 25, no. 1 (Winter 2004): [no pagination].

Libin, Kathryn L. Shanks. "Music, Character, and Social Standing in Jane Austen's *Emma*." *Persuasions* 22 (2000): 15–30.

Litvak, Joseph. "Reading Characters: Self, Society, and Text in *Emma*." *PMLA: Publications of the Modern Language Association of America* 100, no. 5 (October 1985): 763–73.

Lodge, David, ed. *Jane Austen:* Emma: *A Casebook*. Basingstoke: Macmillan, 1991.

MacDonagh, Oliver. *Jane Austen: Real and Imagined Worlds*. New Haven: Yale University Press, 1991.

Mandal, Anthony. *Jane Austen and the Popular Novel: The Determined Author*. Basingstoke: Palgrave Macmillan, 2007.

Marsh, Nicholas. *Jane Austen: The Novels*. New York: St. Martin's Press, 1998.

Martin, Maureen M. "What Does Emma Want? Sovereignty and Sexuality in Austen's *Emma*." *Nineteenth-Century Feminisms* 3 (Fall–Winter 2000): 10–24.

McMaster, Juliet. "The Children in *Emma.*" *Persuasions* 16, no. 14 (December 1992): 62–67.

Meier, Jurg. "Romantic Love as a Narrative Emotion in Jane Austen's *Emma.*" *Prism(s): Essays in Romanticism* 9 (2001): 65–86.

Miller, D. A. *Jane Austen, or, The Secret of Style.* Princeton, N.J.; Oxford: Princeton University Press, 2003.

Morini, Massimiliano. *Jane Austen's Narrative Techniques: A Stylistic and Pragmatic Analysis.* Farnham, England; Burlington, Vt.: Ashgate, 2009.

Morris, Ivor. *Jane Austen and the Interplay of Character.* London; New Brunswick, N.J.: Athlone Press; Somerset, N.J.: Distributed in the United States by Transaction Publishers, 1999.

Perry, Ruth. "Interrupted Friendships in Jane Austen's *Emma.*" *Tulsa Studies in Women's Literature* 5, no. 2 (Fall 1986): 185–202.

Powell, Violet. *A Jane Austen Compendium: The Six Major Novels.* London: Heinemann, 1993.

Rigberg, Lynn. *Jane Austen's Discourse with New Rhetoric.* New York: P. Lang, 1999.

Seeber, Barbara K. *General Consent in Jane Austen: A Study of Dialogism.* Montreal; Ithaca: McGill-Queen's University Press, 2000.

Smith, Peter. "Politics and Religion in Jane Austen's *Emma.*" *Cambridge Quarterly* 26, no. 3 (1997): 219–41.

Stafford, Fiona, ed. *Jane Austen's* Emma: *A Casebook.* Oxford; New York: Oxford University Press, 2007.

Sulloway, Alison G. *Jane Austen and the Province of Womanhood.* Philadelphia: University of Pennsylvania Press, 1989.

Tandon, Bharat. *Jane Austen and the Morality of Conversation.* London: Anthem, 2003.

Tauchert, Ashley. *Romancing Jane Austen: Narrative, Realism, and the Possibility of a Happy Ending.* Basingstoke [England]; New York: Palgrave Macmillan, 2005.

Tobin, Beth Fowkes. "The Moral and Political Economy of Property in Austen's *Emma.*" *Eighteenth-Century Fiction* 2, no. 3 (April 1990): 229–254.

Wenner, Barbara Britton. *Prospect and Refuge in the Landscape of Jane Austen.* Aldershot, England; Burlington, Vt.: Ashgate, 2006.

Acknowledgments

Maaja A. Stewart, "The Fools in Austen's *Emma*." From *Nineteenth-Century Literature* 41, no. 1 (June 1986): 72–86, University of California Press. © 1986 by the Regents of the University of California.

Barbara Z. Thaden, "Figure and Ground: The Receding Heroine in Jane Austen's *Emma*." From *South Atlantic Review* 55, no. 1 (January 1990): 47–62. © 1990 by the *South Atlantic Review*.

Susan Morgan, "Adoring the Girl Next Door: Geography in Austen's Novels." From *Persuasions* 21, no. 1 (Winter 2000): [no pagination]. © 2000 by the Jane Austen Society of North America.

Sarah Emsley, "The Last Pages of *Emma*: Austen's Epithalamium." From *Persuasions* 23 (2001): 188–96. © 2001 by Sarah Emsley.

Isobel Grundy, "Why Do They Talk So Much? How Can We Stand It?" From *The Talk in Jane Austen*, edited by Bruce Stovel and Lynn Weinlos Gregg. © 2002 by the University of Alberta Press.

John Wiltshire, "Comfort, Health and Creativity: A Reading of *Emma*." From *Jane Austen: Introductions and Interventions*, Macmillan/India and Palgrave Macmillan. © 2003, 2006 by John Wiltshire.

Ivor Morris, "The Enigma of Harriet Smith." From *Persuasions* 26, no. 1 (Winter 2005): [no pagination]. © 2005 by the Jane Austen Society of North America.

Juliet McMaster, "*Emma*: The Geography of a Mind." From *Persuasions* 29 (2007): 26–38. © 2007 by Juliet McMaster.

Laura Mooneyham White, "Beyond the Romantic Gypsy: Narrative Disruptions and Ironies in Austen's *Emma*." From *Papers on Language and Literature*, vol. 44, no. 3 (Summer 2008): 305–327. © 2008 by the Board of Trustees, Southern Illinois University at Edwardsville. Reproduced by permission.

Index

Characters in literary works are indexed by first name (if any), followed by the name of the work in parentheses